D. W. Oglesby, RFC®

Concise Encyclopedia
of Investing

Pre-publication
REVIEW . . .

"One of the most effective tools for understanding terms and concepts of personal finance basics. Darren has probably motivated more people to take actual control of their personal financial lives than any other speaker or advisor has in this decade."

Russ Lytle
Regional Director,
Money Concepts

NOTES FOR PROFESSIONAL LIBRARIANS AND LIBRARY USERS

This is an original book title published by Best Business Books®, an imprint of The Haworth Press, Inc. Unless otherwise noted in specific chapters with attribution, materials in this book have not been previously published elsewhere in any format or language.

CONSERVATION AND PRESERVATION NOTES

All books published by The Haworth Press, Inc., and its imprints are printed on certified pH neutral, acid-free book grade paper. This paper meets the minimum requirements of American National Standard for Information Sciences-Permanence of Paper for Printed Material, ANSI Z39.48-1984.

DIGITAL OBJECT IDENTIFIER (DOI) LINKING

The Haworth Press is participating in reference linking for elements of our original books. (For more information on reference linking initiatives, please consult the CrossRef Web site at www.crossref.org.) When citing an element of this book such as a chapter, include the element's Digital Object Identifier (DOI) as the last item of the reference. A Digital Object Identifier is a persistent, authoritative, and unique identifier that a publisher assigns to each element of a book. Because of its persistence, DOIs will enable The Haworth Press and other publishers to link to the element referenced, and the link will not break over time. This will be a great resource in scholarly research.

Concise Encyclopedia
of Investing

BEST BUSINESS BOOKS®
Robert E. Stevens, PhD
David L. Loudon, PhD
Editors in Chief

Doing Business in Mexico: A Practical Guide by Gus Gordon and Thurmon Williams

Employee Assistance Programs in Mananged Care by Norman Winegar

Marketing Your Business: A Guide to Developing a Strategic Marketing Plan by Ronald A. Nykiel

Customer Advisory Boards: A Strategic Tool for Customer Relationship Building by Tony Carter

Fundamentals of Business Marketing Research by David A. Reid and Richard E. Plank

Marketing Management: Text and Cases by David L. Loudon, Robert E. Stevens, and Bruce Wrenn

Selling in the New World of Business by Bob Kimball and Jerold "Buck" Hall

Many Thin Companies: The Change in Customer Dealings and Managers Since September 11, 2001 by Tony Carter

The Book on Management by Bob Kimball

The Concise Encyclopedia of Advertising by Kenneth E. Clow and Donald Baack

Application Service Providers in Business by Luisa Focacci, Robert J. Mockler, and Marc E. Gartenfeld

The Concise Handbook of Management: A Practitioner's Approach by Jonathan T. Scott

The Marketing Research Guide, Second Edition by Robert E. Stevens, Bruce Wrenn, Philip K. Sherwood, and Morris E. Ruddick

Marketing Planning Guide, Third Edition by Robert E. Stevens, David L. Loudon, Bruce Wrenn, and Phylis Mansfield

Concise Encyclopedia of Church and Religious Organization Marketing by Robert E. Stevens, David L. Loudon, Bruce Wrenn, and Henry Cole

Market Opportunity Analysis: Text and Cases by Robert E. Stevens, Philip K. Sherwood, J. Paul Dunn, and David L. Loudon

The Economics of Competition: The Race to Monopoly by George G. Djolov

Concise Encyclopedia of Real Estate Business Terms by Bill Roark and Ryan Roark

Marketing Research: Text and Cases, Second Edition by Bruce Wrenn, Robert Stevens, and David Loudon

Concise Encyclopedia of Investing by Darren W. Oglesby

Concise Encyclopedia of Investing

D. W. Oglesby, RFC®

Best Business Books®
An Imprint of The Haworth Press, Inc.
New York • London • Oxford

For more information on this book or to order, visit
http://www.haworthpress.com/store/product.asp?sku=5689

or call 1-800-HAWORTH (800-429-6784) in the United States and Canada
or (607) 722-5857 outside the United States and Canada

or contact orders@HaworthPress.com

Published by

Best Business Books®, an imprint of The Haworth Press, Inc., 10 Alice Street, Binghamton, NY 13904-1580.

PUBLISHER'S NOTE
The development, preparation, and publication of this work has been undertaken with great care. However, the Publisher, employees, editors, and agents of The Haworth Press are not responsible for any errors contained herein or for consequences that may ensue from use of materials or information contained in this work. The Haworth Press is committed to the dissemination of ideas and information according to the highest standards of intellectual freedom and the free exchange of ideas. Statements made and opinions expressed in this publication do not necessarily reflect the views of the Publisher, Directors, management, or staff of The Haworth Press, Inc., or an endorsement by them.

Cover design by Marylouise E. Doyle.

Example of Ticker Tape reprinted with permission by Investopedia.com.

Library of Congress Cataloging-in-Publication Data

Oglesby, D. W. (Darren W.)
   Concise encyclopedia of investing / D.W. Oglesby.
      p. cm.
   Includes bibliographical references and index.
   ISBN-13: 978-0-7890-2343-8 (hard : alk. paper)
   ISBN-10: 0-7890-2343-1 (hard : alk. paper)
   ISBN-13: 978-0-7890-2344-5 (soft : alk. paper)
   ISBN-10: 0-7890-2344-X (soft : alk. paper)
   1. Investments—Encyclopedias. I. Title.

HG4513.O385 2006
332.603—dc22

                                     2006004756

CONTENTS

Preface   ix

Acknowledgments   xi

Alpha   1
Annuity   2
Asset Allocation   2

Beta   4
Bonds   5

Capital Gains   7
Chasing the Market   7
Commodities   8
Common Stocks   9
Convertibles   10

Diversification   12
Dollar Cost Averaging   13
Duration (Bond)   13

Earnings Per Share (EPS)   15
Emerging Markets   16
Employee Stock Ownership Plan (ESOP)   16
Employee Stock Purchase Plan (ESPP)   17
Equivalent Taxable Yield   18
Estate Planning   18

Face Value   20
Fixed-Income Investment   20
401k Plan   21
403b Plan   21
408k Plan   21
Freddie Mac   22
Front-End Load   23
Full-Service Broker   23
Fund Family   23
Fund Manager   24

Fundamental Analysis 24
Future Value Investment 26
Futures Contract 26

Gap Openings 27
General Obligation Bond 27
Ginnie Mae (Pass-Through) 28
Global Depository Receipt (GDR) 28
Good-Til-Canceled (GTC) Order 29
Government National Mortgage Association (GNMA) 29
Government Securities 30
Growth Stock 30
Guaranteed Bond 31
Guaranteed Investment Contract (GIC) 31

Head and Shoulders 32
Hedge Fund 32
Hedging 34
High-Yield Bonds 35

Immediate Annuity 36
Income Statement 37
Index Funds 37
Individual Retirement Account (IRA) 38
Inflation and Investment 38

Lease 40
Life Insurance 40

Market Timing 41
Markets (DOW, NASD, S&P 500, AMEX) 41
Money Market Funds 42
Mortgage-Backed Securities 43
Municipal Bonds 43
Mutual Funds 44

NASDAQ (National Association of Securities Dealers
    Automated Quotations) 46
New York Stock Exchange (NYSE) 47
Nonqualified Retirement Plans 47

Offering 48
Online Broker 48

Open-End Funds   49
Option Contract   49

Pass-Through Security   51
Pension Benefits   51
Postretirement Benefits   51
Precious Metals   52
Preferred Stock   52
Present-Value Investments   53
Price-Earnings (P/E) Ratio   54
Private Mortgage Participation Certificate   55
Producer Price Index (PPI)   55
Public Purpose Bond   56
Put Option   56

Qualified Retirement Plans   57

Ratio   59
Ratio Analysis   59
Real Estate Investment Trust (REIT)   59
Real Rate of Return   60
Retained Earnings   60
Return on Equity (ROE)   60
Risk   61

S&P/TSX Composite Index   63
Savings and Loans (S&L) Association   63
Savings Bonds   63
Securities   64
Securities and Exchange Commission (SEC)   64
Securities Investor Protection Corporation (SIPC)   65
Selling   65
Shareholders   65
Short-Term Investments   66
Speculator   66
State Regulators   66
Stock   66
Stock Index   67
STRIPS   67
Systematic Risk   67

Tax   69
Tax-Deferred Retirement Accounts   70
Tax Reform Act of 1986   70
Term Life Insurance   71
Ticker Tape   71
Treasury Bills (T-Bills)   72
Treasury Bonds (T-Bonds)   72
Treasury Inflation-Protected Securities (TIPS)   73
Treasury Notes (T-Notes)   73
Treasury Securities   74
Treasury Stock   74
Trusts and Loans   75

Unemployment Rate   76
Unit Investment Trust (UIT)   76

Variable Annuity   77
Variable Life Insurance   77

Wilshire Total Market Index   78
Withholding Tax   78

Yield   79
Yield-to-Maturity   79

Zero-Coupon Bonds   80
Zero-Coupon Convertibles   80

Bibliography   81

Index   85

Preface

The *Concise Encyclopedia of Investing* is for financially and non-financially savvy individuals, business owners, and investors who want to learn more about basic financial concepts. It introduces standard techniques and recent advances in a practical, intuitive way. The encyclopedia conveys complex topics using simple terminology, and the emphasis throughout is on the terms people use when working with personal investments or in business situations.

The *Concise Encyclopedia of Investing* will help readers sharpen their knowledge of investment terminology. In its various entries, I have attempted to convey my overall knowledge of investment situations from working with individual investors during the past ten years. This experience has convinced me that financial techniques and concepts need not be abstract or obtuse but should be broken down so that the average investor can understand and use them.

The *Concise Encyclopedia of Investing* has been written to make available essential information to anyone interested in discovering the world of investments. It contains concise explanations of key terms from the complex world of finance and investment, with numerous examples. It covers issues of practical importance to new investors and offers advice on where a potential investor should look for case-specific information.

ABOUT THE AUTHOR

Darren Wayne Oglesby, RFC®, joined Money Concepts in 1995 as a President by opening the first Money Concepts Financial Planning Center in the state of Louisiana. In 1996, he became the Regional Vice President for the state of Louisiana and was named Rookie Financial Advisor of the Year. He was named the International Network's Financial Planner of the Year for 2001, 2002, and 2003. As a result of the tremendous financial success he has helped his clients achieve, he ranks second out of over 3,000 advisors worldwide and is regularly asked to speak nationwide to his peers on how he and his team have built one of the most successful financial advisory practices in the firm's history.

Mr. Oglesby and staff specialize in working with retirees to help them manage their assets during their retirement years and then transfer them to their heirs. He also presents educational seminars on a regular basis and writes articles for local newspapers and magazines. He is most noted for his commentary on the live radio talk show, "The Money Concepts Show" on Monday mornings on KMLB AM Talk Radio.

Acknowledgments

I am indebted to David Loudon, professor of marketing at Stamford University, Alabama, and Robert Stevens, John Massey Professor of Business at Southeastern Oklahoma State University, Durant, Oklahoma, for their insightful reviews and assistance in producing this book. They did an exceptional job.

I also want to thank my beautiful wife Tracy, my son Cason, and my daughtor Cameron, my parents Wayne and Linda, and my in-laws Steve and Pennie for their inspiration, support, and patience. Finally, I want to express my appreciation to Michael Echols, Director of Public Relations, and the entire team at Oglesby Financial Group for all of their hard work and support in the development of our successful practice. Without them, this book would not have been possible.

Concise Encyclopedia of Investing
© 2007 by The Haworth Press, Inc. All rights reserved.
doi:10.1300/5689_b

A

ALPHA

Alpha is a mathematical estimate of the return expected from an investment's inherent value, such as the rate of growth in earnings per share. Alpha is mainly used to describe the factors that affect the performance of an individual's investment—for example, the individual's skill in selecting stocks. In addition, alpha is an alternative investment intended to reduce market risk.

Alpha is determined by establishing a quantitative model that will yield its value. In other words, a computer-generated model calculates alpha.

Alpha has become part of modern portfolio theory aimed at dividing into constituent parts the sources of risk, identifying additional return opportunities, and creating a diversified portfolio, which can be highly beneficial. It is designed to study the ways an individual or institution can outperform the market and to allow individuals and institutions to expand their sources of performance. A portfolio with a positive alpha is expected to perform better than the index return

Alpha consequently has become the new investing trend. Universities have predicted that more than 50 percent of an individual portfolio will consist of "alternative" sources of investments (stocks) as a result of the search for new strategies and for asset types that are growing and will continue to grow.

Example

An individual has invested in a particular trust fund with a certain expected return, but somehow the benchmark has failed to perform as anticipated. That person can expand his or her portfolio and invest in a new type of asset, such as timber, that has been proven to give a greater return in the market.

Concise Encyclopedia of Investing
© 2007 by The Haworth Press, Inc. All rights reserved.
doi:10.1300/5689_01

ANNUITY

Annuity is an arrangment whereby an individual pays a twelve-monthly premium in exchange for a future stream of annual payments beginning at a set age and continuing until death. An annuity is a type of investment that pays out benefits in installments over a set period of time. Annuities are often used as a source of extra income for people in retirement.

An annuity it is not life insurance because it is not an accumulation used to protect an individual against financial loss. Instead, it is used as a protection against economic difficulties a person may experience in retirement.

Annuities can be classified according to the way they are paid (single premium or installments), the disposition of proceeds (life annuity with no refund, guaranteed-minimum annuity, annuity certain, and temporary life annuity), the start date of benefits (immediate and deferred annuity), and the method used to calculate benefits (fixed-rate and variable annuities).

Example

Thinking about the future, an individual pays an annual premium to an insurance company and both parties agree on the arrangements for future payments to the individual. The insurance company will establish a flow of annual payments at a set age (e.g., sixty-five years old) that continue until the death of the individual.

ASSET ALLOCATION

Assets are cash or tangible material goods with financial value. Asset allocation is the way that institutions' and individuals' funds are distributed among the major categories of investment, such as investments, stocks, real estate, collectibles, cash, and bonds. The distribution will vary according to the goals of the company or individual. Traditionally, these assets are grouped into subcategories such as government, corporate bonds, and stocks.

The way companies and individuals decide to distribute their assets becomes the most important element in determining the level of returns. The purpose of asset allocation is to allow the individual to balance the probable rewards from an investment against the risk associated with that investment. Consequently, asset allocation is a way for individuals and companies to eliminate some percentage of risk when they consider a particular investment.

The two main types of assets are *current* and *fixed*. *Current assets* include cash and other assets that may be converted into cash when they are sold or which could be used in the future in regular business operations. Current assets could include liquid assets—cash, or any item that can become cash, real estate (home, condominium, summer property), personal possessions (automobiles, jewelry), and investment assets (funds set aside for long-term financial needs). Fixed assets include any physical facility used by a company for manufacture, such as storage space, display, and distribution.

Assets can be allocated in two ways: a *stable policy* and an *active strategy*. A stable policy, as the term suggests, is one whereby an individual, based on income needs, pursues a strategy with little risk involved. He or she assigns an equal amount to each asset, eliminating the need to make decisions and allowing a more stable return over an extended period. Active strategy asks an individual to establish his or her tolerance for risk and long-term goals; then he or she allocates the percentage of money he or she will invest in each asset. With this strategy the person will anticipate the performance (profit or loss) of each asset over the year to determine the increase or decrease in the investment to be made in that asset. Compared with a stable policy, an active strategy involves a higher risk and requires a good knowledge of the financial markets.

Example

A married couple is creating a personal portfolio. If they have a steady income that permits a certain percentage of risk and they consider, based on news and statistics, that the coffee market is growing, the couple can consider investing between 35 and 65 percent in coffee stocks.

$\boxed{B}$

BETA

As opposed to alpha, which concerns itself with the individual's earnings, beta focuses on market risks, mainly on the behavior of stocks. It is a way to calculate how the price of a specific stock changes in the market. Studies have proven that traditional investments do not always perform better than the market and that they are affected by specific market conditions; this finding led to risk analysis and, thus, beta.

Beta estimates average risk premiums and unsystematic risk. However, it is important to be aware that the beta can be measured with error resulting in a bias in the information provided regarding a particular stock and its change with respect to the market.

Example

An individual has invested in mutual funds for the past year; however, market conditions have decreased the expected return because of the devaluation of such stock. Consequently, the expected return of 40 percent will in actuality be a return of 30 percent.

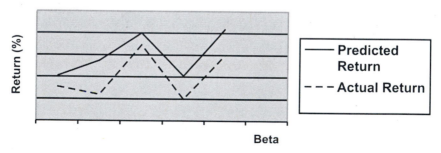

FIGURE 1. Beta measurements.

BONDS

Bonds are fixed-income securities with a maturity of one or more years; thus, they are the sum unpaid, issued for a specific period of time. Some bonds pay a fixed amount of interest twice a year, and this interest earned represents the difference between the face value of the bond (the amount the bondholder will receive at the bond's maturity) and the price paid. This interest rate (also known as the yield on maturity), which will be paid every six months, is set by the company or institution. In addition, the higher the interest rate is the lower the bond's price is and vice versa. Corporations or different governmental institutions such as local governments, U.S. government, and companies often issue bonds. Bonds are often *callable,* which means that the issuer has the right to buy the bond back from the bondholder at a preset price before maturity. Bonds often do not constitute a risky investment; however, this will vary according to the type of bond.

The major types of bonds are government, municipal, corporate, mortgage, and pass-through securities. The first three are the most frequently issued types. *Government bonds* include treasury bills, treasury notes, treasury bonds, and U.S. government savings bonds; these bonds are used to pay off national debt or origin government activities. The interest earned on this type of bond is exempt from state, but not federal, income taxes in the United States. *Municipal bonds* are used to fund highway repairs, build new schools, improve city facilities, and parks. These bonds have a certain risk level and thus always carry bond ratings. The interest earned on municipal bonds is exempt from U.S. federal taxes but not from state taxes. *Corporate bonds* are issued by companies to cover expansion and operating expenses. The common types of corporate bonds are

1. *Asset-backed or mortgage bonds:* bonds backed up by specific assets, such as real estate and machinery
2. *Debenture bonds:* the most common type; they have no collateral to protect them and the only thing a bondholder has is the guarantee that the issuer will pay back
3. *Floating rate bonds:* periodic adjustments are made according to market interest rates
4. *Pre-refunded bonds:* repayment is guaranteed by funds from another bond issue, usually U.S. treasury securities

5. *Subordinated debentures:* higher coupon rates than debentures issued by the same company
6. *Zero-coupon bonds:* very popular with some investors because they have no coupon rates and as maturity approaches their price is higher

Example

An investor has acquired a bond with a $10,000 value and a set interest rate of 8.5 percent; the investor will receive $850 per year. However, the amount will be divided semiannually (850 ÷ 2 = 425) until the maturity date (i.e., until the date on which the company has agreed to repay the amount invested).

C

CAPITAL GAINS

Capital gain occurs when the money realized from a particular asset exceeds the original retail price; for example, the sale of stocks, bonds, or real estate. There can be two types of gain: *long-term gains* and *short-term gains*. Long-term gains consist in the assets held for eighteen months and the maximum tax rate on the capital gain is 20 percent, assets such as art, antiques, stamps, and other collectibles are still at a 28 percent tax rate. However those in the 15 percent bracket pay a 10 percent tax on long-term gains. Short-term gains are those earned on investments held for less than eighteen months and are subject to regular income tax rates.

Examples

1. An individual or company purchases a house, maintains it for a period of twelve months or more, and then sells it for a profit earns a long-term gain.
2. A small clothing business that purchases a stock of winter clothes and successfully sells every item during the winter season has a short-term gain subject to federal tax rates.

CHASING THE MARKET

"Chasing the market" is an unorthodox method in which an investor follows the market, buying a stock after a rise and selling after a fall. Traditionally, finance companies or investors do not advise individuals to follow such a method due to its inconsistency and the high degree of risk.

Similar to whipsaw, which consists of buying a stock before rapid drops and selling before rapid growth, the technique of chasing the market puts an individual's investments into a volatile, constantly changing market of drops and rises, resulting in a high risk of loss. For instance, an individual who owns a particular stock, sees the value of the stock decreasing suddenly, and decides to sell it. That person might be losing more than he or she would by waiting a little longer to see the reaction of the market, because the stock might unexpectedly increase in value.

Example

An investor wants to buy a share of a particular stock at a value of $25; when the investor suddenly realizes that this stock is increasing its value, he or she will buy at $27, before the price gets any higher. Alternatively, the owner of a particular stock bought at an original price of $15 realizes that the value of the stock is declining; the investor quickly sells the share before the value decreases further.

COMMODITIES

Commodities are contracts to buy or sell goods such as cotton, corn, wheat, coffee, cocoa, and tobacco with other investors in a future date. Historically, according to the *Commodity Exchange Act,* commodities include all agricultural products with the exception of onions; however, commodities have come to include power and energy, metals and mined products, technology, agriculture, and other specialized markets.

Commodities do not pay interest or dividends, and the return is determined merely by the commodity's demand. Consequently, commodities are considered a very risky investment; as quickly as returns can exceed the amount invested, they can turn into losses. Commodities are often traded on what is known as a futures market. Commodities trading is rather complex: no one can rely on previous performance beause the market continually changes.

Example

An apple farmer made a 50 percent return in the year 2000 on his crop of Washington apples. However, in 2001 the farmer risks the cost of production if he produces as many apples as in 2000 without

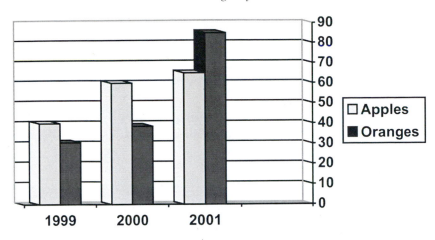

FIGURE 2. Commodities example.

certainty whether the demand for Washington apples will be as high as it was in the previous year. In 2001, the market reports that oranges are the commodity of the year and that apples are in second place in terms of value. The farmer consequently does not realize the same high return as in 2000.

COMMON STOCKS

Companies often offer common stocks to the public to finance their business and ongoing activities. Common stocks are shares representing the capital of a company and the complete claim to such profits as remain after the holders of preferences have been paid. They also confer a voting privilege on the stockholder in terms of selecting the board of directors, who exercise overall control of the company and represent its shareholders.

Common stockholders are also given preemptive rights, which allow them to maintain their relative ownership of the company if it distributes a later offer of stocks. In addition, preemptive rights give shareholders the right, but not obligation, to purchase more shares.

The position of common stockholders in relation to the dividends and control of an enterprise may leave little or nothing to the common shareholders if the company's operation is low. Consequently, common shareholders lack secured stability because they receive their shares only after all other shareholders, such as creditors, have received their profits, making them the lowest priority when a business enterprise is shut down.

Some companies divide their common stock into two classes, A and B. Both have similar privileges, but Class B usually has the voting right.

CONVERTIBLES

Also known as deferred equities, convertibles are an exchangeable number of securities, usually bonds or preferred shares, which can be converted into common stock at a predeclared price. They are used by all types of companies either as convertible bonds or as convertible preferreds.

A convertible tends to perform well whenever the stock market is strong, but when the market turns down so does the interest in convertibles. Furthermore, the key element of any convertible is the conversion privilege. Conversion privilege states the exact time when the debenture can be converted.

Convertibles are ideal for investors who want a greater appreciation potential than bonds give and higher income than common stocks may offer. Moreover, for issuers, convertibles are usually planned to enhance the marketability of bond or preferred share.

Among the advantages of investing in convertibles is that they reduce downside risk and at the same time provide an upward price potential comparable to that of the firm's common stock. Another benefit is that the current income from bond interest normally exceeds the income from the dividends that would be paid with a comparable investment on the underlying common stock. However, there are some disadvantages in the investing of convertibles. Buying the convertible instead of directly owing the underlying common stock means and investor has to renounce to some potential profits.

By combining the characteristics of stocks and bonds into one security, convertibles offer some risk protection and at times considerable increases in price potential.

Convertibles are subject to the same brokerage fees and taxes as corporate debt and convertible preferreds trade at the same cost as any preferred does or common stocks.

D

DIVERSIFICATION

Diversification can be classified as *individual*—spreading risk by placing assets in several categories of investment, such as stocks, bonds, mutual funds, and precious metals; and *corporate*—investing in different business areas, similar to a conglomerate.

Diversification is an important concept when an individual invests in assets. It refers to investing your assets among a variety of funds that have different levels of risk and return.

Diversification allows individuals to create a portfolio strategy designed to reduce the risk by combining a variety of investments (bonds, stocks, etc.). The main goal of diversification is then to reduce the risk in a person's portfolio, thus reducing the risk of losing money in a single investment. Different types of investments tend to behave differently under similar or the same market conditions.

Thus, diversification follows the traditional saying "Don't put all your eggs in one basket." This is an elementary rule of investing. Professionals agree that the investment market is not risk-free. With diversification, if one stock does not perform well, another might compensate for the loss.

In addition, diversification requires time and energy in order to track a number of stocks and bonds. Some individuals buy a range of mutual funds and do not have to worry about the market; instead, the money is managed by a group of professionals. Mutual funds are investment companies that take money from a number of investors and determine an investment strategy that fits the goals of the fund.

Example

A couple who has decided to create a diversified asset portfolio but lacks the knowledge and time should call a local financial group and acquire a mutual fund managed by a number of financial advisors.

DOLLAR COST AVERAGING

Dollar cost averaging is financial planning whereby a series of fixed dollar amounts are invested in a particular stock during a regular period of time. Divisions of capital, instead of a large sum of money, are invested in set intervals over a period of time. For this plan to work, an investor must maintain the discipline of making regular investments.

The goal is to increase the value of the stock. The price of the investment, however, will vary over time. If the price of the stock declines, the investor will buy more stocks, but if the price augments, a smaller amount of shares will be acquired. Investors often use this approach to avoid the traditional problem of buying a particular stock high and then selling it low.

Example

Most companies in the United States allow their employees to buy shares of company stock. A set amount is taken out of an employee's check over an extended period of time, and when the employee retires the company pays the interest earned on his or her stock share. (*See* BONDS.)

DURATION (BOND)

Duration of a bond is the measure of the bond price volatility by measuring "the length of time" of a bond stated in years. It is commonly defined as the weighted average term to maturity of a security's cash flows, where the weights are the present value of each cash flow as a percentage of the security's price. In other words, duration is a weighted measure of the length of time the bond will pay out.

The duration of a bond can be calculated in four ways: Macaulay duration, modified duration, effective duration, and key-rate duration. The calculation most often used is Macaulay's formula.

$$\text{Macaulay Duration} = \frac{\sum_{t=1}^{n} \frac{t*C}{(1+i)^t} + \frac{n*M}{(1+i)^n}}{C*\left\{\frac{1-\left[\frac{1}{(1+i)^n}\right]}{i}\right\} + \frac{M}{(1+i)^n}},$$

where n = number of cash flows; t = time to maturity; C = cash flow; i = required yield; and M = maturity (par) value.

Duration provides an approximation of a bond's percentage price change for a 1 percent change in interest rates. Duration is a helpful tool because it allows an investor to calculate the possible interest rate risk when a bond is purchased. However, although this method works well for short-term changes in interest rates, it does not work well for long-term changes in interest rates because it assumes a parallel shift in the yield curve, which will not apply for a long-term investment due to the fluctuating market. Consequently, many financial institutions and magazines such as *Business Week* emphasize that several factors must be considered regarding duration.

First, duration calculations must include any embedded options, including any call and put provisions a bond may have, because these embedded options affect the shape price/yield function. Second, the price of a bond is never linear; in fact, it is generally concave (or positively *convex*). Thus, duration will overestimate the price changes for a given change in yield in the long term; it works only to calculate short changes in yield. Finally, duration presumes a parallel shift in the yield, which is an unrealistic assumption since yield does not have a parallel shift. Thus, the price changes of two bonds with the same duration and different cash flows can differ depending on the curve.

An investor can be certain that rules apply to duration. First, with the exception of *zero-coupon bonds* and some fixed- income securities, the duration of the bond will always be lower that its maturity. Second, with the same exceptions, bonds with a higher coupon rate will have a lower duration, and vice versa. Third, as the market yield increases (decreases), the duration of the bond decreases (increases).

Example

The value of a bond with a duration of three years will decline by approximately 3 percent for each 1 percent increase in interest rates and rise by apporximately 3 percent for each 1 percent decrease.

E

EARNINGS PER SHARE (EPS)

Earnings per share is also referred to as *profits per share*. Traditionally used to measure corporate value, EPS is the profit gained from each share within the market. In other words, EPS interprets the total profit of a corporation on a per-share basis and provides a measure of the amount of earnings available to stockholders. The profit used to calculate EPS is the profit that belongs to the shareholders. EPS is considered "fully diluted" when the common stock equivalents (convertible bonds, preferred stock, warrants, and rights) have been exchanged into common stock.

EPS is calculated by subtracting from net income the preferred dividends (which have to be subtracted before paying the stockholders) and then dividing by the number of outstanding common shares:

$$\text{Earnings Per Share} = \frac{\text{Net profit after taxes} - \text{preferred dividends paid}}{\text{Total number of shares of common stocked issued}}.$$

Even though most companies use this method, some argue that it is not the best indicator of a company's earnings due to the fact that it excludes risk, investment requirements, time value of money is overlooked, and dividend policy is not contemplated, among other things. Stockholders follow the magnitude of EPS because it represents the amount that the company has earned in terms of the shares of common stock.

Although EPS can be calculated for the previous year, the current year, or a future year, only the past-year calculation will be accurate; the present and future calculations are considered estimates.

Example

If company X reports a net profit of $25,000, pays $5,000 in dividends to preferred shareholders, and has 5,000 shares of common stock issued, it will have an EPS of $4.00 ([25,000 − 5,000]/5,000]).

EMERGING MARKETS

An emerging market, by definition, is a country that attempts to transform its economy by improving its operation to the levels of the world's more advanced nations. In other words, emerging markets are financial markets of developing countries. They allow economies to become more competitive and more open to international investors.

Emerging markets are the result of the financial support programs of international institutions with the primary goal of creating stronger economies.

Some investors favor emerging markets because they offer the prospect of achieving a high rate of return in a short period of time. However, political situations and unexpected economical changes can make emerging markets a risky investment because the values of stocks and currency can change drastically from one day to the next.

Examples

Some emerging markets are: Mexico, South Africa, China, and Lithuania, among others.

EMPLOYEE STOCK OWNERSHIP PLAN (ESOP)

In the United States, ESOP is a type of defined contribution plan that buys and holds company stock. ESOPs are often used in closely held companies to buy part or all of the shares of the existing owners, but they are also used in public companies.

An ESOP is a form of tax-qualified employee benefit plan in which most or all of the assets are invested in the stock of the employer. Similar to profit-sharing and 401k plans, an ESOP usually includes at least all full-time employees meeting certain age and service requirements. The company contributes its own shares to the plan, cash to buy its own stock (often from an existing owner), or, most common, money borrowd to buy stock (with the company repaying the loan). Thus, employees do not actually buy shares in an ESOP. Employees are gradually vested in their accounts and receive their benefits when they leave the company (although there may be distributions prior to that).

ESOPs are most commonly used to provide a market for the shares of the departing owners of successful closely held companies, to motivate and reward employees, or to take advantage of incentives to borrow money for acquiring new assets.

ESOPs cannot be used in partnerships or most professional corporations, but they can be used in S corporations. Private companies have to buy shares from departing employees, which can become a significant investment. Moreover, the cost of setting up an ESOP is very high—$15,000 to 20,000 for basic plans.

Among the advantages of ESOPs are that (1) they provide a friendly buyer for the stock; (2) the owner retains control of the business; (3) the employees participate in the growth of the company; and (4) the owner can defer the tax on capital gains realized when shares are sold to the ESOP if the profits are reinvested in qualified replacement property within a given period.

EMPLOYEE STOCK PURCHASE PLAN (ESPP)

Similar to a stock option plan, an ESPP allows employees to buy stock, usually through payroll deductions, over a three- to twenty-seven-month "offering period." The price is generally discounted by up to 15 percent from the market price. Frequently, employees can choose to buy stock at a discount from the lower of the prices either at the beginning or the end of the ESPP offering period, which can increase the discount still further. As with a stock option, after purchasing the stock, the employee can sell it for a quick profit or hold onto it for a while. Unlike stock options, the discounted price built into most ESPPs means that employees can profit even if the stock price goes down. Companies usually set up ESPPs as tax-qualified Section 423 plans (allowing employees under U.S. tax law to purchase stock at a discount from the fair market value without any taxes being owed on the discount at the time of purchase), which means that almost all full-time employees with two years or more of service must be allowed to participate.

An employee can leave the plan at any time; however, it is always wise to check the documents signed for any rules applying to withdrawals.

EQUIVALENT TAXABLE YIELD

Equivalent taxable yield is the yield that must be offered on a taxable bond issue to give the same after-tax yield as a tax-exempt issue; moreover, it is a comparison of the taxable yield on a corporate or government bond and the tax-free yield on a municipal bond. Depending on the investor's tax bracket, the after-tax return may be greater on a municipal bond than on a corporate bond that has a higher interest rate. The equivalent taxable yield is equal to the municipal yield divided by 100 percent minus the tax bracket.

Example

An investor in a 30 percent tax bracket who has a 10 percent municipal bond has an equivalent taxable yield of 14.2 percent (10 percent/70 percent).

ESTATE PLANNING

Estate planning is the process of considering alternatives and making legally effective preparations that will meet individuals' wishes in case something happens to them or the people around them (e.g., spouses, children). Estate planning prepares for the administration and disposition of an estate when the owner dies. It does not consist simply of drawing up of a will and setting up trusts; it also minimizes estate taxes and fees, perhaps by passing property to heirs before death, and ensures an individual's wishes regarding health care and or funeral arrangements are followed.

A person's estate includes real estate, cash, bank accounts, stocks and bonds, jewelry, automobiles, employee benefits (e.g., pension plan), and anything else that the person owns and controls.

Estate planning is a process usually carried out by a group of skilled professionals that may include an attorney, an accountant, a life insurance agent, a trust officer, and a financial planner.

Examples

1. A man who has a serious disease and knows that in a period of time he will be unable to make decisions regarding his health desig-

nates, through his estate plan, a close relative (wife, son, daughter) to make decisions for him. He also states in the plan that this person can be authorized to "pull the plug" if needed.

2. An eighty-year-old woman has decided that before she dies she will divide up her estate. She creates an estate plan where all of her family members receive their inheritance before her death.

F

FACE VALUE

Known also as *par value, nominal value,* and *principal amount,* face value is the stated principal amount that appears on the front, or face, of a note or certificate. Corporate bonds usually have face values of $1,000, municipal bonds of $5,000, and government bonds of $10,000. Unlike the bond's value, which changes with the market, the face value does not change. Moreover, it does not matter whether at maturity the price of the bond has increased or decreased: the amount paid will be the face value. Face value, in other words, is the amount that the issuer agrees to pay at the maturity date.

If a bond is retired before maturity, bondholders may receive a slight premium over face value. It is also the amount on which interest payments are calculated.

Example

A 10 percent bond with a face value of $1,000 will pay the investor $100 per year.

FIXED-INCOME INVESTMENT

This is an investment that pays a fixed rate of return. The term is generally used to refer to government, corporate, or municipal bonds, which pay a set rate of interest over a given period of time.

Such investments are usually advantageous in a time of low inflation, but otherwise can become rather risky. They are affected primarily by interest rate risk: as the interest rate changes, the prices of these securities fluctuate, decreasing with rising interest rates and increasing with low rates. This type of investment is also subject to two types of risk: interest rate risk and credit risk. The return to an individual from such investments is not assured, and thus they do not guarantee a stable portfolio.

401K PLAN

A 401k plan is a retirement plan that allows employees in private companies to make contributions of pretax dollars; it is a qualified plan established by employers to which eligible employees can make salary deferral (salary reduction) contributions on a post- and/or pretax basis. Employers can make matching or nonelective contributions to the plan on behalf of eligible employees and can also add a profit-sharing feature to the plan. Earnings accrue on a tax-deferred basis.

Caps placed by regulations and/or the plan usually limit the percentage of salary deferral contributions. Restrictions apply to how and when an employee can withdraw assets, and penalties may apply if the amount is withdrawn before the age of fifty-nine.

Plans that allow participants to direct their own investments provide a core group of investment products for them to choose from. Otherwise, professionals hired by the employer direct investments.

403B PLAN

This is a retirement plan for university, civil government, and not-for-profit organization employees, with the same characteristics and benefits as a 401k plan. According to the IRS regulations, only employees of public schools and tax-exempt organizations exclusively for religious, charitable, scientific, public-safety testing, literary, or educational purposes are allowed to participate.

Employees with a 403b plan have a number of choices, including annuity and variable annuity contracts with insurance companies, a custodial account made up of mutual funds, and retirement income accounts for churches. Participants set aside money on a pretax basis through a salary reduction agreement with their employer. The money is then directed to a financial institution selected by the employer. The money grows with tax deferred until retirement and is taxed as ordinary income on withdrawal.

408K PLAN

Also known as a SARSEP plan (salary reduction simplified employee pension), a 408k plan is a simplified alternative to a 401k plan aimed mainly at companies with twenty-five or fewer employees. It allows employees to contribute pretax dollars through salary reduction. The law prohibited new SARSEP plans from being established after 1996, and state or local governments, any of their political subdivisions or agencies, and tax-exempt organizations cannot use a SARSEP plan. However, employers with established SARSEPs prior to January 1, 1997, can continue to maintain them.

A SARSEP is funded by employee contributions (salary deferrals) and also sometimes by nonelective contributions from the employer (employer contributions that are made to each eligible employee's account).

A SARSEP is easy to set up and operate. A company or individual has to fill out Form 5305A-SEP and call a financial institution to get things started. A SARSEP plan is very practical: the administrative costs and requirements are low and contribution requirements are flexible. However, some discrimination rules apply so that contributions do not favor certain employees. Contributions are 25 percent of each employee's compensation, with a $40,000 limit per employee.

FREDDIE MAC

Freddie Mac (Federal Home Loan Mortgage Corporations) is a stockholder-owned corporation created by Congress with the intention of stabilizing the mortgage markets and increasing opportunities for homeownership and affordable rental housing.

Freddie Mac purchases single-family and multifamily residential mortgages and mortgage-related securities in the secondary market and then packages them into securities that can be sold to any investor. Through this process the corporation ensures the flow of funds to provide low- to middle-income homeowners with lower housing costs and access to home financing. However, not all loans are packaged into securities; some are retained within the corporation's portfolio.

The Web site (www.freddiemac.com) provides information regarding the corporation's history, resources for home ownership, and advice on doing business with Freddie Mac.

FRONT-END LOAD

Also known as a *load fund,* a front-end load is a sales charge paid when an individual buys a new investment, usually mutual funds but also a limited partnership, annuity, or insurance policy. This charge, or commission, is applied at the time of purchase, rather than at the time of sale as in the case of back-end loads. The load is clubbed with the first payment made by an investor, so the total initial payment will be higher than the later payments.

The purpose of this charge is to cover administrative expenses and transaction costs.

FULL-SERVICE BROKER

A full-service broker is a broker who in addition to smoothing the progress of transactions, makes available to clients a full selection of services. Unlike discount or online brokers (who carry out trades but do not provide any form of research information or advice), full-service brokers advise on which stocks, bonds, commodities, and mutual funds an individual should buy or sell. They may also advise on financial planning, tax shelters, income-limited partnerships, and new issues of stocks. As a result, a full-service broker will charge higher commissions than a discount or online broker.

FUND FAMILY

Also known as a *family of funds,* a fund family is a group of funds that have different objectives but are all administered by a *single* investment management company. Individuals can switch their money from one fund to another within the same family according to their needs or changes in the market. Even though the switching is free, transferring money from one fund to another may have tax implications.

The major no-load fund families include: American Century, Dreyfus, Fidelity, T. Rowe Price, Scudder, Strong, and Vanguard. Fund families are also sponsored by key brokerage houses, including Merrill Lynch, Smith Barney, and Paine Webber.

FUND MANAGER

A fund manager is the individual responsible for making the decisions regarding an investor's portfolio of investments. A fund manager is also in charge of overseeing the pool of money invested in mutual funds, pension funds, insurance funds, or bank-pooled funds. The manager has the job of maximizing the return (income or growth) and attaining the minimum level of risk.

It is important for an investor to know a fund manager's style and history of investments. Detailed information is generally available to the public via the Fund Report Overview, the company, or fund representatives.

FUNDAMENTAL ANALYSIS

Fundamental analysis is the study of the financial affairs of a business to better understand its nature and operating characteristics. Fundamental analysis takes account of economic factors, industry-specific trends, capital market conditions, and company-specific data and qualities. Fundamental analysis takes two main forms: quantitative analysis, where economic or company-specific numerical data are analyzed, and qualitative analysis, which examines less tangible concepts such as technology strength and management effectiveness. The main tenet is that the value of a stock is influenced by the performance of the company that issued it.

Fundamental analysis begins with a historical analysis of the company's financial strength (known also as *company analysis*). In this process, the investor studies the financial statements of the company (past records of assets, earnings, sales, products, management, and markets) and examines the firm's strengths and weaknesses in order to predict future trends.

After doing such study the fundamental analyst then creates a financial statement that is given to investors to help them better understand the company's financial situation. Financial statements are of three types: balance sheet (company assets, liabilities, and shareholders' equity), income statement (summary of the operating results of the firm), and statement of cash flows (summary of the firm's cash flows and other elements that can change the cash situation).

A fundamental analysis considers only those variables that are directly related to the company itself, rather than the price and movement of stocks in the market.

XXX Industries Balance Sheet December 2006	
Assets	
Current assets	
Cash and short-term investments	$ _____
Accounts receivable	$ _____
Inventories	$ _____
Prepaid expenses	$ _____
Total current assests	$ _____
Long-term assets	
Land	$ _____
Buildings	$ _____
Furniture and equipment	$ _____
Other assets	$ _____
Total assets	$ _____
Liabilities and Stockholders' equity	
Current liabilities	
Notes payable	$ _____
Current maturities	$ _____
Taxes on earnings	$ _____
Total current liabilities	$ _____
Long-term debt	$ _____
Stockholders' equity	
Common shares	$ _____
Capital surplus	$ _____
Retained earnings	$ _____
Total stockholders' equity	$ _____
Total liabilities and stockholders' equity	$ _____

FIGURE 3. Example of a balance sheet.

FUTURE VALUE INVESTMENT

Future value investment is the amount to which a current deposit placed in an account paying compound interest will grow over a period of time. Compound interest is interest earned on the principal plus interest earned earlier. It can be calculated daily, weekly, or continuously, depending on the institution. Whereas present value investment in a project stipulates that the project will cover the capital invested, future value investment involves depositing an amount of money, *x*, in a particular account, such as a savings account, in the knowledge that over a certain period this money will increase by the compound interest generated.

Example

Planning for retirement in the year 2025, an investor decides to open an account that generates daily compound interest, with a rate of return of 10 percent. In one year, the investor will have a future value of $1,105.16.

FUTURES CONTRACT

Agreement or commitment to buy or sell a set number of shares of a specific stock, a currency, or a financial instrument during a selected future month at a price agreed upon by the buyer and seller. The buyer and seller set the price using an *open outcry* system. A futures contract is a legally binding promise to complete a transaction; consequently, the parties involved are forced to complete such transaction; however, there are cases when the contract may be sold before the settlement date, which may happen if the trader wants to take a profit or cut a loss. Thus, a futures contract differs from an option because an option is a right to buy or sell, whereas a futures contract does not ensure the right of the buyer to exercise his or her options.

A futures contract is part of a class of securities called *derivatives*. A futures contract is often traded in a futures market. Such markets establish their own contract guidelines covering not only the quantity and quality of the stock but also the delivery procedure and delivery month, or expiration date, which defines the life of the contract. In addition, futures contracts have their own trading hours, and all trading in futures markets is on a margin basis.

G

GAP OPENINGS

Also known as *price gaps,* gap openings occur between the day before and day after of a trading session and are significant price movements of a security or commodity between the two sessions such that there is no overlap in the trading ranges for the two days. Technical analysts who chart gap openings consider them to be significant movements because they are indicators of an overbought or oversold position.

Example

A stock might shoot up from a closing price of $25 per share, marking the high point of a $23 to $25 trading range for that particular day, to begin trading in a $27 to $29 range the next day on the news of a takeover offer.

GENERAL OBLIGATION BOND

Generally abbreviated to *G-O bond,* general oblication bonds are municipal bonds (usually issued in $5,000 denominations) backed by the full faith and credit of the issuer (municipality) and including its taxing and further borrowing powers. They must be serviced in a prompt and timely fashion irrespective of the level of tax income generated by the municipality.

G-O bonds are repaid with general revenue and borrowings, in contrast to the revenue from a specific facility. Caution should be used when buying such bonds because some of these issues are tax-exempt and others are not.

GINNIE MAE (PASS-THROUGH)

This is security backed by a pool of mortgages and guaranteed by the Government National Mortgage Association (GNMA or Ginnie Mae), which passes through to investors the interest and principal payments of homeowners.

Homeowners make their mortgage payments to the bank or savings and loan that originated their mortgage. After deducting its service charge (usually 0.5 percent), the bank forwards the mortgage payments to the pass-through buyers, who may be institutional investors or individuals.

A Ginnie Mae pass-through guarantees that investors will receive timely principal and interest payments even if homeowners do not make mortgage payments on time. However, the rate of principal repayment for investors on a Ginnie Mae pass-through is uncertain. If interest rates fall, the principal will be repaid more quickly, since homeowners will refinance their mortgages. If rates rise, however, the principal will be repaid more slowly, since homeowners will hold on to the underlying mortgages.

The investors in a Ginnie Mae pass-through receive both the principal and the interest from the pool or mortgages.

Three types of Ginnie Mae pass-throughs are available:

1. GNMA 1—securities are single-issuer pools whose certificates pay principal and interest separately.
2. GNMA 2—securities are multiple-issuer pools (called jumbos) that are longer and more geographically diverse than single-issuer pools, with certificate holders receiving aggregate principal and interest payments form a central paying agent.
3. GNMA midgets—certificates backed by fifteen-year fixed-rate mortgages.

GLOBAL DEPOSITORY RECEIPT (GDR)

This is a negotiable certificate held in a bank in one country representing a specific number of shares of a stock traded on the exchange of another country. These receipts or certificates are traded in capital markets around the world, allowing companies from Europe, Asia, the United States, and Latin America to offer their shares in markets other than that of their home country. One advantage is that companies are not limited to increasing their capital from their own country's market. The advantage for local investors is that they do not have to risk buying shares in foreign companies on the company's home exchange; the share price and all dividends are converted into an investor's home currency. However, companies that issue GDRs are not as well established as some conventional Western firms; their stocks tend to be more unpredictable and less liquid.

Some companies in emerging markets such as China and Brazil issue a number of GDRs.

GOOD-TIL-CANCELED (GTC) ORDER

Also known as an *open order,* GTC is an order to buy or sell securities, usually at a particular price, which remains in effect until it is executed or canceled. If a GTC order remains unfilled for an extended time, a broker will periodically confirm that its customer still wants the transaction to occur if the stock reaches the target price.

Example

An investor places a limit order to to buy fifty shares of a particular stock at a price of $10, knowing that the stock is currently selling at $11. After clearing all similar orders, the broker will execute the order if the price of the stock falls to $10 or less.

GOVERNMENT NATIONAL MORTGAGE ASSOCIATION (GNMA)

GNMA, also named Ginnie Mae, is an issuer of mortgage-backed bonds and it is a wholly owned government corporation within the Department of Housing and Urban Development.

GNMA puts together a pool of home mortgages and then issues securities in the amount of the total mortgage pool. After doing so, GNMA guarantees, with the full faith and credit of the U.S. government, that investors will receive full and timely principal and interest payments, even if the mortgages in the pool are not paid on a timely basis. Thus, GNMA's main goal is to ensure liquidity for U.S. government-insured mortgages, including those insured by the Federal Housing Administration (FHA), the Veterans Administration (VA), and the Rural Housing Administration (RHA). GNMA does not issue, sell, or buy mortgage-backed securities or purchase mortgage loans. GNMA makes housing affordable and allows mortgage lenders to obtain a better price for their loans in the secondary market.

Other guarantors or issuers of loans eligible as collateral for Ginnie Mae MBS include the Department of Housing and Urban Development's Office of Public and Indian Housing (PIH).

GOVERNMENT SECURITIES

Also known as *agency securities,* government securities are created by the government to raise money or funds for its expenses. They include treasury bills, notes, and bonds.

Such securities have high credit ratings but are not considered to be government obligations; thus, they are not directly backed by the full faith and credit of the government as treasuries are. Agencies that issue such bonds include the Resolution Funding Corporation (REF-CORP) and the Federal Land Bank.

GROWTH STOCK

Growth stock is the stock of a company with rapid earnings growth that is expected to continue to grow at high levels. Growth stocks are riskier investments than average stocks because they usually sport higher price/earnings ratios. They also generally pay little or nothing in dividends, as the company's rapid growth requires that its earnings be held and reinvested.

Owing to their potential for dramatic price appreciation, growth stocks appeal primarily to investors who are seeking capital gains rather than dividend income.

Growth stocks include Microsoft, Boeing, Franklin Resources, Motorola, and Intel.

GUARANTEED BOND

A guaranteed bond is a corporate bond in which principal and interest are guaranteed by an entity other than the issuer, such as an insurance company. Guaranteed bonds are in effect debenture (unsecured) bonds of the guarantor. However, if the guarantor has stronger credit than the issuer, the bonds have greater value.

Such bonds are nearly always railroad bonds, but they may also arise from a parent-subsidiary relationship, where bonds are issued by the subsidiary with the parent's guarantee.

GUARANTEED INVESTMENT CONTRACT (GIC)

GICs are insurance contracts that guarantee the owner principal repayment and a fixed or floating interest rate for a predetermined period of time, traditionally one to ten years. A GIC is an obligation issued in return for a payment by an investor. GICs are typically issued by insurance companies and marketed to institutions qualified for favorable tax status under federal laws.

They work similarly to certificates of deposit, with the exception that they are sold by insurance companies. Their terms vary greatly, but they usually offer a relatively high initial guaranteed return and impose some restrictions on the investor's ability to withdraw funds.

A similar contract offered by a bank is called a bank investment contract (BIC) or a bank deposit agreement (BDA).

H

HEAD AND SHOULDERS

Head and shoulders is a technical pattern used to describe a pattern in a market or security that rises to a peak then declines, then the price rises above a former peak then declines, and finally the price rises again but not to the previous peak and declines once again. This trend is normally seen when markets move between highs or lows passing a securities equilibrium point.

The peaks that are seen first and third are considered the shoulders. The second peak seen is the head. The indication from a head and shoulders pattern is considered to be a bearish indicator.

HEDGE FUND

A hedge fund is a private investment partnership, owned by wealthy individuals and institutions, that is allowed to use aggressive strategies unavailable to mutual funds, including short selling, leverage, program trading, swaps, arbitrage, and derivatives. Since they are restricted by law to less than 100 investors, the minimum hedge-fund investment is typically $1 million.

1. *Hedge funds pursue absolute returns.* Hedge funds aim to generate positive returns and protect gains in any market. This is the critical difference between hedge funds and mutual funds. Whereas hedge funds seek positive returns in falling markets, conventional "long-only" mutual funds and pension funds (which can only make money when markets go up) typically aim only to outperform a benchmark index. Even if asset prices fall, traditional fund managers continue to focus on just beating a declining benchmark. Hedge funds are popular because most investors would prefer a consistent risk-averse 10 to 13 percent return every year to the pattern of up 30 percent one year, minus 15 percent the next, then plus 5 percent, then minus 20 percent,

say, that one gets with equity funds with high systematic risk and stock market correlation. Good hedge funds generate absolute returns, making consistent attractive profits for investors year in, year out, without references to or hiding behind relative performance.

2. *Hedge funds are skill-based investments.* The belief underpinning all forms of alternative investment is that capital growth can be generated in a variety of ways in markets. Unlike in traditional investment approaches, which depend mainly on asset appreciation for their performance, the primary drivers of performance in alternative investments, including hedge funds, are the skill, expertise and actions of their managers. By combining specialized knowledge of markets with defined investment processes, hedge fund managers aim to identify and successfully exploit various market inefficiencies and opportunities. Most hedge fund managers seek to exploit market opportunities with identifiable and understandable causes and origins. The pursuit of absolute performance is highly dependent on the skill of the investment manager, who may take advantage of pricing anomalies between related securities (arbitrage), engage in "momentum" investing to capture market trends, or utilize expert knowledge of markets and industries to capture profit opportunities that arise from uncertainty, volatility, or political events. A hedge fund manager's skill can contribute 80 percent of the returns, and the movements of underlying markets only 20 percent;, the reverse is true of a traditional mutual fund, as the best manager can lose money all day long in a bad market.

3. *Hedge funds have total investment flexibility.* Hedge funds have the flexibility to invest in any available asset class or financial instrument and to employ a variety of clearly defined investment styles, strategies, and techniques in diverse markets. This freedom affords managers rich opportunities to generate growth and protect capital in falling, rising, and unstable markets. Hedge fund managers are unencumbered by the sorts of regulatory and methodological restrictions that characterize traditional fund management, such as restrictions on going to cash. The ability to use derivatives, arbitrage techniques, and, importantly, short selling (selling assets one does not own in the expectation of buying them back at a lower price) allows hedge funds to profit handsomely from a hostile market.

4. *Fund managers' and investors' interests are the same.* Given the confidence and belief hedge fund managers must have in their strat-

egy and investment process, they typically commit a significant portion of their net worth to the funds they manage. Investors have the confidence that comes from knowing that the manager's economic interests and risk and return objectives are aligned with their own, which is not always the case in other investments. Managers are also paid according to performance rather than assets under management, which attracts the top minds in the financial world to hedge fund management, and their objective is the same as the objective of every investor—to make money consistently year after year. In most funds, any previous losses must be recouped and new highs reached before the performance fee is paid again (known as the high-water mark).

5. *They diversify and enhance total portfolio returns.* Hedge funds can serve as powerful diversification tools. They can make a valuable contribution to the risk/reward profile of any investment portfolio because their performance is not correlated with that of other asset classes. This means that allocating investments to hedge funds will allow a portfolio to make more money, more consistently, even when other assets such as stocks, bonds, and real estate are performing poorly. The inclusion of hedge funds in a portfolio of traditional assets results in lower portfolio volatility and increased returns—that is, improved risk-adjusted returns—through the application of modern portfolio theory.

HEDGING

Hedging is simply a combination of two or more securities into a single investment position to reduce risk using call options, put options, short selling, or futures contracts. A hedge can help lock in existing profits. Examples are a position in a futures market to offset a position held in a cash market, holding a security and selling that security short, and a call option against a shorted stock. Hedging can involve buying stock and simultaneously buying a put on the same stock, or it can consist of selling some stock short and then buying a call. Hedges come in many forms, some of which are very sophisticated and others very simple. All are used for the same basic reason: to earn or protect a profit without exposing the investor to excessive loss. A perfect hedge eliminates the possibility of a future gain or loss. An imperfect hedge insures against a portion of the loss.

HIGH-YIELD BONDS

Also called junk bonds, these are the lowest-quality bonds. High-yield bonds have credit ratings below BBB and are considered speculative because they have a greater chance of default than investment-grade bonds. High-yield bonds are usually issued by smaller companies without long track records or by companies with questionable credit ratings. To compensate for the additional risk, issuers offer higher yields than those on investment-grade bonds.

I

IMMEDIATE ANNUITY

This is a contract bought with a single payment to an insurance company that has a specific payout plan and will reimburse the annuitant (the person to whom future payments on an annuity are directed) either immediately (this traditionally means thirty days after the deposit) or in certain cases at a deferred date.

In addition to being based on a statistical analysis carried out by the insurance company, the amount invested in an immediate annuity will vary according to the annuitant's gender and age. Most immediate annuity plans also calculate the annuitant's life expectancy, and based on this the insurance company and the annuitant go over a number of *period certain annuities* (five year, ten year, fifteen year, and twenty year). These specify the length of time for which the individual will receive payments, which are usually made monthly, ceasing if the annuitant passes away before the end of the specified period. After agreeing to an immediate annuity, the annuitant cannot change the date.

Immediate annuities are safe investments that have little or no accumulation phase and can help secure the financial future of an individual by locking in a guaranteed income stream. They are simple to manage because the annuitant does not have to watch the market constantly or report interest or dividends. Moreover, the interest rate used by insurance companies to calculate the immediate annuity income is higher than Treasury rates, and immediate annuities allow the postponement of tax payments. Thus, immediate annuities are often a good idea for people retiring from employment, pension terminations, and credit enhancement.

The most traditional immediate annuities are known by different names: *single-life, straight-life, life-only,* or *nonrefund* annuity.

The funds used to acquire immediate annuities are classified as either qualified and unqualified, depending on their tax status. Qualified funds are those that have come from a corporate-sponsored retirement plan, from individual arrangements such as IRSs, SEPs, or from life insurance exchanges, and the whole payment is taxable as income. Unqualified immediate annuities are purchased with funds that have not enjoyed any tax-shelter status, for example, money from the sale of a house, inheritance, business, mutual funds, and life insurance settlements.

Example

A couple thinking about retirement sell their house. To secure a stable income, they decide to invest the money. Knowing that an investment in stocks can be risky because of fluctuations in the market, they decide to purchase a contract for an immediate annuity. Suppose the property was sold for $125,000 and the couple decide to save half of the amount. They contact an annuity specialist, who can inform them about the terms of the investment and coverage. The retiring couple decide that a single-life fifteen-year period certain will be the most appropriate option and that they want to receive their first payment within a year. In addition, they agree that if one partner dies before the contract expires, the other will receive the payments until the end of the fifteen-year period.

INCOME STATEMENT

An income statement, also known as an *operating statement, statement of profit and loss,* or *income and expense statement,* is a summary of the revenues, costs, and expenses of a company. It provides a financial report on the firm that usually constitutes part of the financial statement of the company. An income statement is drawn up during a particular period and usually covers a year of operation.

INDEX FUNDS

An index is a hypothetical portfolio of stocks selected according to some established criteria. An index fund is a mutual fund that buys and holds securities that match a broad-based market index such as the S&P 500. An index fund tries to match, rather than beat, the return or performance of an established index or general market.

Index funds offer diversification and low management fees, thus they allow anyone to participate in the stock market. In addition, index funds produce very little taxable income each year, and thus investors consider them to be tax-shelter investments.

The best-known index fund is the Vanguard 500, which tracks the S&P 500.

INDIVIDUAL RETIREMENT ACCOUNT (IRA)

An IRA is an investment account opened through a bank, brokerage firm, or mutual fund. IRAs are called "individual" retirement accounts because they are opened them under an individual's own name; joint IRAs are not available, even for married couples. IRAs come in several forms: traditional IRAs, Roth IRAs, SIMPLE IRAs, and simplified employee pension plan (SEP) IRAs.

Traditional and Roth IRAs are accounts created by individual taxpayers, who can contribute 100 percent of their compensation (i.e., self-employment income for sole proprietors and partners) up to a specific amount. Contributions to a traditional IRA may be tax deductible, depending on the taxpayer's income, tax-filing status, and coverage by an employer-sponsored retirement plan. Roth IRA contributions are not tax deductible. *SEPs and SIMPLEs* are retirement plans established by employers. Individual participants make contributions to SEP and SIMPLE IRAs.

INFLATION AND INVESTMENT

Inflation (a rise in the prices of goods and services) and *investment* (the use of capital to create more money) are terms that often come together, because inflation affects investments differently, depending on the type of securities in a portfolio.

As the rate of earnings from a particular investment increases, so will inflation. Fixed-income investors feel the impact of inflation most.

Some securities guarantee that inflation will not consume the return of the investor. Among these are Treasury Inflation-Protected

Securities (TIPS), which are special types of Treasury notes or bonds. TIPS are similar to any other Treasury bonds in making interest payments every six months, but the principal and coupon payments are tied to the Consumer Price Index (CPI) and are increased to compensate for any inflation.

Example

During a time of war the demand for certain products is higher; the cost of goods and services increases, and thus inflation rises. The dollar may lose value agains other currencies and an investment in stocks and bonds will not be as reliable as before.

L

LEASE

A lease is a written contract that grants the lessee or tenant the use of real estate, equipment, or some other fixed asset for a set period of time in exchange for a payment.

Leases can vary in duration and take several forms, depending on what is being rented: operating lease, financial lease, capital lease, renter's lease, direct financing lease, open-end lease, sales-type lease, and true lease, among others.

Example

A family moving to a new city decides to rent an apartment. After they find an appropriate apartment, the family sits down with the owner to talk about the rent and the lease contract. The family has to leave a deposit and a first month's rent and has to lease the place for a one-year period. If they need to break the contract, they must give thirty days' notice to the lessor's office. In addition, the owner agrees to contact them when the lease has reached its grace period to say whether they can renew the lease agreement.

LIFE INSURANCE

Life insurance guarantees an explicit sum of money to a designated beneficiary or beneficiaries upon the death of the insured or to the insured if he or she lives beyond a particular age. Life insurance protects the family or dependents of the policyholder after the policyholder's death.

The three main categories are term, universal, and whole life insurance. Term life insurance is the simplest and least expensive. It has no cash value and it has the option to pay a specific sum of money to a beneficiary or beneficiaries.

M

MARKET TIMING

Market timing is the procedure in which the individual or corporation analyzes and identifies the state of the economy/market and assesses the changes of its course. Thus, through this process of observation and analysis, the individual makes the decisions on when to buy or sell securities, based on these economic factors.

Through the use of fundamental or technical indicators the investor can switch from different types of funds as the market changes. Even though it is hard to declare if a certain investment will increase its growth, investors follow market timing because it allows them to invest funds into stocks back and forth according to the current state of the economy/market.

Example

An individual with an investment in a stock fund with company X sees that the fund is less stable than it was. The investor can switch the investment to a money fund that promises an improved return. Such swithces can be made many times, according to the available information on the state of the economy or markets.

MARKETS (DOW, NASD, S&P 500, AMEX)

AMEX (American Stock Exchange): The second-largest stock exchange by the number of listed companies. By dollar volume of trading, AMEX is smaller than the Midwest and the Pacific regional exchanges. AMEX handles only 2 percent of the total annual dollar volume of shares, whereas the New York Stock Exchange (NYSE) handles 90 percent. Consequently, the NYSE is home to the best-known companies in the world. However, the stock market changed dramatically when *NASDAQ* took over AMEX, which will make it a strong competitor for the NYSE in years to come.

Dow Jones Averages: This is the oldest and most followed measure of stock market performance, with four components: (1) an industrial average based on thirty stocks, (2) a transportation average based on twenty stocks, (3) a utilities average based on fifteen stocks, and (4) a composite average based on all sixty-five stocks. Financial critics argue that the average of blue chips claimed by Dow hardly represents the behavior of the market. However, the facts show that Dow reflects objectively other stock market measures.

NASD (National Association of Securities Dealers): This is an association comprised of all the brokers and dealers who participate in the over-the-counter market. The NASD is a self-regulatory organization that polices the activities of brokers and dealers to ensure its standards are upheld. The Securities and Exchange Commission (SEC) supervises the activities of the association to protect investors from deceitful activities and to guard investors against potential exploitation by investment advisors who sell their services to the public.

Standard & Poor's (S&P) Indexes: Similar to Dow Jones averages, S&P indexes are used to depict the overall performance of the market. However, they include more stocks. The most popular is S&P 500, which is based on 500 stocks covering all large stocks from the NYSE and some of the main stocks on AMEX and the over-the-counter market. Even though S&P has eight basic indexes, it is the S&P 500 that is commonly followed by the financial media and reported not only in the major financial journals but also in most popular newspapers in the United States. The value of S&P is lower than that of Dow, not because it consists of less valuable stocks but because of the methods used to calculate the measures.

MONEY MARKET FUNDS

MMFs, also known as *money funds,* are open-end mutual funds that pool the capital of an investor and use it to invest only in short-term money market instruments such as certificates of deposit, commercial paper, repurchase agreements, government securities, and other safe and liquid securities.

MMFs are highly liquid, low-risk, investment vehicles practically protected from capital loss. They are just as liquid as checking or savings accounts, and they are often viewed as profitable, safe, and convenient. They usually offer the convenience of checking privileges and the management fee is less that 1 percent of an investor's assets. An MMFs net asset value remains constant at $1 per share, but the interest rate does fluctuate.

MMFs come in three types: (1) general-purpose money funds, (2) government securities money funds, and (3) tax-exempt money funds. They are part of fund families, allowing an individual investor to switch money from one fund to another. Most MMFs are not federally insured, but some have private insurance.

MORTGAGE-BACKED SECURITIES

These types of securities are usually sold in minimum denominations of $25,000. The average life of an issue is relatively short (perhaps eight to ten years) because many of the pooled mortgages are paid off early. The interest is paid monthly rather than semiannually. The monthly payments received by bondholders are made up of both principal and interest. As the principal portion of the payment represents return of capital, it is tax free.

MUNICIPAL BONDS

Also known as *munis,* municipal bonds are issued by a state, city, country, local government, or other political subdivision to raise capital for infrastructure projects, such as construction of toll roads, highways, and hospitals. Whether such bonds are tax deductible depends on their purpose. If a bond has a public purpose, it is tax exempt; bonds for a private purpose are taxable unless specifically exempted.

Municipal bonds are considered safer than corporate bonds because the issuer is less likely to go bankrupt than a private company.

Municipal bonds are held manily by individual investors, especially those with a hefty tax burden. They are often issued as serial obligations, which means that the issue is broken into a series of small bonds, each with its own maturity date and coupon.

Municipal bonds come in two forms: (1) general obligation, and (2) revenue bonds. *General obligation* bonds are backed by the full faith, credit, and taxing power of the issuer. They must be serviced in a rapid and timely fashion irrelevant of the level of tax income received by the municipality. *Revenue bonds* are serviced by the income generated from specific income-producing projects. The holder of a revenue bond is required to pay principal and interest only if a sufficient level of revenue is generated.

Individuals often have a difficult time deciding which type of municipal bond to invest in, but a formula can help them decide which type of fixed-income investment will provide the greatest after-tax return:

$$\text{Taxable equivalent yield} = \frac{\text{yield of maturity bond}}{1 - \text{federal tax rate}}$$

Municipal bonds usually come in $5,000 par value and usually require a minimum investment of $25,000.

MUTUAL FUNDS

These are funds operated by an investment company that invests shareholders' money in a diversified portfolio of securities. Mutual funds raise money by selling shares to the public. Then, with this money, they purchase investment vehicles, most commonly cash, stock, and bonds. By law, mutual funds cannot invest in commodities and their derivatives or in real estate. Other restrictions should be made clear to an investor before accepting his or her investment.

Most mutual funds are open-end funds. Although certain people refer to close-end funds as mutual funds, they are actually investment trusts.

Shareholders are free to sell their shares any time; however, they need to be aware that the price of a share in a mutual fund will fluctuate daily.

For an individual interested in creating a diversified portfolio, mutual funds have benefits such as diversification and professional management (a professional manager will forecast the future performance of investments). In addition, mutual funds offer choice, liquidity, and convenience, but they charge fees and often require a minimum investment. Moreover, as mutual funds are corporations under

U.S. law, they are subject to a special set of regulations and accounting and tax rules.

Many types of mutual funds exist: asset allocation funds, growth funds, aggressive growth funds, equity-income funds, balanced funds, growth-investment funds, bond funds, money market funds, index funds, sector funds, socially responsible funds, and international funds, among others.

Example

An investor wants to create a more diversified portfolio of thirty stocks to improve her credit history. However, she is unable to come up with a sum of $30,000 to invest $1,000 per stock. To achieve her goal, she opens a mutual fund for $1,000 and a professional fund manager integrates her money into a pool of money from several investors and invests the total pool a large portfolio of stocks and bonds.

$$\boxed{N}$$

NASDAQ (NATIONAL ASSOCIATION OF SECURITIES DEALERS AUTOMATED QUOTATIONS)

NASDAQ is an electronic quotation system, run by the National Association of Securities Dealers (NASD), that provides security quotes to brokers, traders, and market makers and allows buyers and sellers of stocks to be paired automatically. Unlike the New York Stock Exchange, NASDAQ has no central trading location; all trading is carried out over a network of computers and telephones.

Investors place orders for particular stocks. These are sent out electronically on NASDAQ, where market makers list their buy and sell prices. The price is settled and the transaction is executed electronically.

NASDAQ lists nearly 41,000 companies and is home to the top U.S. growth companies as well as international companies. Thus, NASDAQ allows many market participants to trade through its electronic communications networks, increasing competition with other countries.

NASDAQ has two markets: (1) The NASDAQ National Market, which is the market for its largest and most actively traded securities, among them Microsoft and Intel, and (2) the NASDAQ Small Cap Market for emerging growth companies, which move up to the NASDAQ National Market as they become established.

To participate in NASDAQ, an investor must subscribe to it. Subscription fees are classed as professional and nonprofessional. Investors go through a number of tests to determine their status as professional or nonprofessional.

For more information, go to www.nasdaq.com or http://www.nasdaqtrader.com/.

NEW YORK STOCK EXCHANGE (NYSE)

Also known as *the Big Board* or *the Exchange,* NYSE is one of the most important stock exchanges in the United States and the largest in the world. It is operated by the not-for-profit corporation New York Stock Exchange, Inc., which has its main building at the corner of Wall Street in New York City.

The NYSE is the exchange with the most rigorous requirements for listing, and it is where the majority of the largest and most established U.S. companies are listed. It is considered old-fashioned because unlike NASDAQ, the NYSE operates on face-to-face contact between buyers and sellers in a particular physical location.

On the trading floor is one podium for each of the exchange's stocks. Brokers (people who represent the buyer or seller at the time of a stock exchange) interested in buying or selling a particular stock gather around the appropriate podium, where a NYSE employee facilitates negotiations and buys those stocks no one else will. The NYSE employee shouts out prices to strike a deal. This is called the *open outcry system* and it usually generates fair market pricing.

For more information go to http://www.nyse.com.

NONQUALIFIED RETIREMENT PLANS

These are plans designed to enable employees and owner-employees to save significant sums for retirement without most of the restrictions imposed on qualified retirement plans by ERIS and tax codes. Nonqualified retirement plans allow an employer to choose a group of employees to participate in and receive the benefits from the plan, porviding a way to reward select employees and incentivize other employees in the company. An example of this type of plan is the Well's Fargo Non-Qualified Retirement Program.

O

OFFERING

Also known as a *public offering,* this is the *offering* of new securities to the public through an underwriting at a public offering price that has been agreed upon by the issuer and its investment bankers or a syndicate made up by several investment bankers. The offering can be made only after the issue has been registered with the Securities and Exchange Commission (SEC). Offerings can also be secondary distributions of previously issued stocks.

ONLINE BROKER

An online broker, also known as an *electronic broker* or *cyber broker,* provides trading services to customers, including full-service, discount, and deep-discount brokers, over the Internet.

Online brokers usually charge flat rates (5 to 10 percent) for transactions up to 1,000 shares, with additional fees for larger or more complex orders—a fraction of the amounts charged by full-service brokers. Today, fees of $5 to $7 per online trade are common and one of the main reasons online investments continue to grow.

Even though the fees are minimal, an investor should consider the downside of online brokers, which is the risk of technical interruptions of service and the possibility that low-publicized transaction costs may hide additional expenses associated with the executions of the third market.

Many banks and institutions now make online brokerage services available to their clients, in addition to the major online brokers such as Merrill Lynch, Paine Webber, and Smith Barney.

OPEN-END FUNDS

Most mutual funds are open-end funds. They are referred to as open-end because no time or number limit is placed on the new shares that they can issue or redeem. Generally, companies an create open-end funds to raise money by selling shares in the fund to the public. Mutual funds then use the money to purchase various investment vehicles, such as stocks and bonds. Shareholders they receive an equity position in the fund and in each of its underlying securities.

The price of an open-end fund is determined by the net asset value (NAV). The number of shares outstanding does not affect the value of each individual share; in other words, the price is determined solely by the change in process of the stocks or bonds the fund owns, not by the size of the fund itself.

Open-end fund shareholders are free to sell their shares at any time, although the price of a share will fluctuate daily depending upon the performance of the fund.

If sales charges are imposed, the fund is referred as a load fund; otherwise, it is a no-load fund. Although some open-end funds have no sales charges, brokerages may charge commissions for the purchase of any type of fund (load or no-load), and fees might be associated with the fund, such as maintenance fees in an IRA account for no-load funds.

Investors agree that open-end funds are suitable for regular incomes because they usually give the option of receiving dividends on a monthly, quarterly, semiannual, or annual basis. Moreover, they are suitable for those looking for an increase or appreciation in their investments, and they can also provide a fair amount of protection against inflation.

Most well-known funds, such as Fidelity's Magellan and Vanguard's S&P 500, are open-end funds.

OPTION CONTRACT

An option contract gives its holder the right, not the obligation, to buy or sell a fixed number of shares (usually 100 shares) of a particular stock, commodity, currency, index, or debt at a fixed price on or before a specific time (usually three, six, or nine months hence).

Each option contract has a buyer (the holder) and a seller (the writer) and is settled at the discretion of the buyer. If settlement would involve a cash flow from the seller to the buyer, the buyer will exercise his or her option and receive a payment from the seller. In contrast, if the arrangement would involve a cash flow from the buyer to the seller, the buyer will choose not to exercise the option and no funds will change hands. That is, the buyer will exercise the option only when it is in his or her interest to do so, meaning that the buyer will receive either a cash flow or nothing when the contract matures.

Buyers hope that the stock's price will go up (if they bought a call) or down (if they bought a put) by enough to provide a profit at the moment of sale. The risk is that the price will hold steady or move in the opposite direction, in which case the price paid is completely lost.

Option contracts take many forms, but the best-known forms are *call options* and *put options*. A call option gives the holder the right to buy a particular asset at a specified price (the *strike price*) within a specified period of time. A put option gives the holder the right to sell a particular asset at a specified price within a specified period of time.

The last date on which an option can be exercised is its expiration date. The two standard forms of exercise are *American exercise* and *European exercise.* With American exercise, the option can be exercised at any time up to expiration. With European exercise, the option can be exercised only on the expiration date. With a third form of exercise, *Bermudan exercise,* the option can be exercised on a few specific dates before the expiration date.

Option contracts are most frequently regarded as either *leverage* or *protection.* As leverage, options allow the holder to control equity in a limited capacity for a fraction of what the shares would cost. As protection, options can guard against price fluctuations in the near term because they provide the underlying stock at a fixed price for a limited time.

Options are very complex and require a great deal of observation and maintenance.

P

PASS-THROUGH SECURITY

Also known as a *mortgage pass-through security,* a pass-through security represents pooled debt obligations rearranged as shares or participation certificates in the pool. The cash flow from the pool is passed through to the security holder (government agency, investors, or investment banks) as monthly payments of principal, interest, and prepayments. This is the predominant type of mortgage-backed security traded in the secondary market.

Pass-throughs are usually sold in minimum denominations of $25,000, issued by Ginnie Mae, Freddie Mac, and others.

PENSION BENEFITS

These are benefits due to a worker at the point of retirement. A company creates an employer-sponsored retirement plan. Retirement benefits are based on a formula. Investment risk and portfolio management are entirely under the control of the company. Restrictions are placed on when and how a participant can withdraw funds without serious consequences.

POSTRETIREMENT BENEFITS

Postretirement benefits include all types of retirement health and welfare benefits other than pensions. Examples are medical coverage, dental coverage, life insurance, group legal services, and other benefits that continue after an employee retires. The most common form of postretirement benefit is health care.

Formerly, companies accounted for benefit payments made after the employee retired on a pay-as-you-go or cash basis, but with postretirement benefits companies are instead required to recognize the estimated future cost of providing postretirement benefits.

Information on postretirement benefits can be found in footnotes accompanying a company's financial statements that describe the benefits offered, show their expense and changes in benefit obligation calculations, and describe any assumptions made.

PRECIOUS METALS

Precious metals include gold, silver, platinum, gems, and palladium. Precious metals are used as a form of investment because of their value in different markets. They are considered tangible investments and tend to perform well during high inflation periods.

The market for tangible investments and thus their liquidity fluctuates, but precious metals are considered less risky because they are portable.

PREFERRED STOCK

Also known as *preference shares,* preference stocks act like bonds but confer additional rights to those conferred by common stock. Preferred stocks represent partial ownership of a company, although some companies do not allow preferred-stock shareholders any of the voting rights of holders of common stock.

A preferred stock pays a fixed dividend that does not fluctuate; however, the company does not have to pay this dividend if it lacks the financial means to do so. Preferred shares are more common in private companies, where it is useful to distinguish between control of and the economic interest in the company.

The main benefit of owning preferred stock is that the investor has a greater claim on the company's assets than those who hold common stock. Preferred shareholders always receive their dividends first and in the event the company goes broke, preferred shareholders are paid off before common stockholders.

In most instances, preferred stock comes with a conversion clause permitting it to be exchanged for common shares. Preferred stocks require that the investors check on the conversion premium, or gap, between the conversion price and the market price of the common, because a large gap means limited appreciation for the preferred, and little chance of conversion in the near future.

Institutions, rather than individuals, usually buy preferred stocks; however, individuals can gain access to them through a mutual fund.

The four main types of preferred stocks are cumulative, noncumulative, participating, and convertible (plus a subcategory of nonconvertible preferred stocks).

1. *Cumulative preferred.* This is the most issued form; dividends accumulate and must be paid before common dividends.
2. *Noncumulative preferred.* Preferred stock in which unpaid dividends do not accrue. On noncumulative preferred stocks, omitted dividends will never be paid off as opposed to cumulative preferred stocks.
3. *Participating preferred.* In addition to a regular dividend, participating preferreds pay a participating dividend when common stocks exceed a specified amount; they also confer the right to additional dividends under certain circumstances.
4. *Convertible preferred.* Stocks that may be exchanged into common shares at the owner's or the company's specific prices or rates.
5. *Nonconvertible preferred.* Term describing a preferred stock that cannot be converted into common shares, as opposed to convertible preferred stocks.

The majority of preferred stocks fall into the nonconvertible subcategory; thus, many financial institutions recommend this type of preferred stock to corporations rathern than individuals. Nonconvertible preferred stock remains exceptional in perpetuity and trades in a similar way to stocks. Utilities are the best example of nonconvertible preferred stock issuers.

PRESENT-VALUE INVESTMENTS

Present value is the value today of a sum to be received at some future date, the inverse future value. For present-value investments, the capital spent exceeds the value of the present cost of the investment.

A present-value investment project should exceed the price paid for the investor to recoup the funds used to buy or support the project.

By identifying the net cash flows and the cost of a present-value investment, an individual can estimate the percentage of the cost of funds, or the discount cash flow.

Example

An investor examines a variety of projects with potential for a high level of success and demand, for example, technology, a building, or a new store opening in a foreign country. Based on this potential, the investor chooses one project, e.g., Internet cafés in Central America, where it is possible to calculate the cash flow and the cost of the investment and to estimate that after a period of one year this project will successfully refund the cost of capital.

PRICE-EARNINGS (P/E) RATIO

Also called *earnings multiple,* the P/E ratio is the measure used most often to show investors how expensive a stock is. It is calculated as the latest closing price, or market capitalization, divided by the past twelve months' after-tax earnings per share. Alternatively, it may be computed with leading earnings (earnings projected for the coming twelve-month period) when it is called a *leading P/E.* The value is the same whether the calculation is performed for the entire company or on a per-share basis.

The P/E ratio is very useful for comparing one firm with others from the same industry or, in certain cases, different industries. A company with a higher P/E ratio might be expected to produce a higher and more consistent earnings growth than one with a lower P/E ratio. However, it is also possible that the stock is simply more expensive than other stocks.

In the past, stock experts maintained that a good P/E ratio falls somewhere between fifteen and thirty. The investment community tends to view a company with an increasing P/E ratio as more and more speculative because young, fast-growing companies are riskier to trade than low P/E stocks, and in some cases their stocks are becoming overvalued. Low P/E stocks tend to be in low-growth or mature industries and have higher yields than high P/E stocks, which often pay no dividends.

A company's P/E ratio changes every day as the stock price fluctuates. Thus, in some cases it is difficult to determine whether the P/E ratio of a company is high or low.

The trailing P/E ratio of a company is listed along with stock price and trading activity in daily newspapers.

Example

A stock trades for $60 per share and the company has earnings per share of $3. Dividing the price by the trailing earning yields a P/E ratio of 20.

PRIVATE MORTGAGE PARTICIPATION CERTIFICATE

This is a pass-through representing an interest in a pool of instruments such as mortgage-backed securities; also a security that represents an interest in mortgages. Private mortgage participation certificates are the most common type of pass-through security; they operate either as direct issues of pass-through securities or as issues structured with a trustee. With *direct issues,* the originator of the mortgage issues pass-through securities to investors, giving them beneficial ownership of the underlying mortgage. *The trustee structure* introduces a third party that can act as an additional safeguard; in this case, beneficial ownership of the mortgage passes to the trustee and the trustee in turn issues pass-through securities that represent interests in the underlying mortgage. Finally, the party originating the mortgage markets the securities.

PRODUCER PRICE INDEX (PPI)

The PPI is a comprehensive index of wholesale price changes in the economy. The U.S. Bureau of Labor Statistics calculates the index monthly. Its components are broken down by industry, sector, commodity, and processing stage. As producers pay for things that will eventually be consumed, the PPI is regarded as an indicator of what lies ahead in terms of inflationary pressures.

PUBLIC PURPOSE BOND

Public purpose bonds are also known as *public activity, traditional government purpose,* and *essential purpose bonds.* Public purpose bonds are a type of municipal bond exempt from federal income taxes as long as they provide no more than a 10 percent benefit to private parties and as long as no more than either 5 percent of the proceeds or $5 million is used for loans to private parties. Thus, the benefits to private individuals are very small.

Public purpose bonds are used for the constructions of roads, libraries, government buildings, and similar projects.

PUT OPTION

Put option is an option contract that gives the owner the right, but not the obligation, to sell a specified number of securities, commodities, or financial instruments at a specified price (strike price) by a certain date. The put option buyer gains these rights in return for payment of an option premium; the seller grants these rights in return for this premium and assumes the related obligations.

The best-known put option is the stock option, which is the option to sell a stock in a particular company. However, options are also traded on many other assets, including gold, interest rates, and crude oil.

Example

An investor enters into a contract to sell an option in a particular company for $60 on December 13, 2006. If the company's share price is $50 on that date, the investor has the right to sell. However, if the share price is $70, the investor will not exercise the option because he could sell it in the open market for $70 and make more profit.

QUALIFIED RETIREMENT PLANS

Qualified retirement plans are the plans approved by the IRS that allow for tax-deferred increase of investment income. Individual retirement accounts (IRAs), Keogh plans, SEP, simple IRAs, 401k plans, and 403b plans, and 457 plans are examples of qualified retirement plans.

IRAs are similar to any account opened with a bank, credit union, stockbroker, mutual fund, or insurance company. When the documents are filled out the account is designated an IRA and the institution becomes the trustee. Anyone can apply for an IRA. The tax depends on a number of factors; hence the variety of IRAs available (e.g., traditional IRAs, nondeductible IRAs, Roth IRAs). Their requirements differ, but all are accounts that encourage an individual to save for retirement by protecting the investment income from income taxes.

Keogh Plans were introduced as part of the Self-Employed Individuals Tax Retirement Act. They allow anyone who is self-employed full- or part-time to set up tax-deferred retirement plans for themselves and employees. They can be treated as deductions from taxable income, reducing the tax bills of self-employed individuals. The maximum contribution is 20 percent of income earned. Keogh plans are not limited to self-employed people; they can also be used by professionals with a job on the side, for instance, a psychologist who works full-time as a school counselor and gives therapy on the weekend. Keogh accounts can be opened with banks, insurance companies, brokerage houses, mutual funds, and other financial institutions.

SEPs are similar to Keogh plans. They are aimed at small-business owners, primarily those with *no employees,* who want a plan that is easy to set up and administer. They have the same dollar amount contribution cap as Keogh plans, but the contribution rate is less generous: only 15 percent of income earned.

401k or salary reduction plans are the most popular supplementary retirement plans among employees. They are a form of contribution plan, in essence giving employees the option of diverting a portion of their salaries to a company-sponsored, tax-sheltered savings account. The earnings put into the plan accumulate tax free. For example, a manager who earns $75,000 per year wants to contribute $10,000 to a company 401k plan. This contribution reduces the manager's income to $65,000 per year and, assuming he or she is in the 25 percent tax bracket, lowers his or her federal tax bill by $2,500 ($10,000 \times 0.25$).

403b plans offer many of the same features as 401k plans. They are commonly used for workers in public schools, colleges, universities, nonprofit hospitals, and similar institutions.

457 plans are similar to 401k plans. They are used for employees who work for the state, local government, or tax-exempt organizations.

R

RATIO

Ratio is one value divided by another, and it provides the representative of the value of one quantity in comparison with another.

RATIO ANALYSIS

Ratio analysis is a method of analysis used in making credit and investment judgments. Ratio analysis studies the relationship between various financial variables.

REAL ESTATE INVESTMENT TRUST (REIT)

A REIT is a company usually traded publicly, that manages a portfolio of real estate to earn profits for shareholders. REITs can also invest in loans, such as mortgages. They do not necessarily increase and decrease in value along with the broader market.

REITs offer several benefits to shareholders. First, they are highly liquid, unlike traditional real estate, and can be traded on major exchanges, making it easier to buy and sell REIT shares. Second, REITs enable investors to have a stake in nonresidential properties as well. Third, REITs have no minimum investment limit. Fourth, REITs allow shareholders to invest in a professionally managed portfolio of real estate properties. Finally, REITs receive special tax considerations and usually offer investors high yields, which are paid in the form of dividends no matter how the shares perform.

Equity REITs invest in and own properties; thus, their revenues come from rent. *Mortgage REITs* deal in investment in and ownership of property mortgages. With mortgage REITs, investors loan money for mortgages to owners of real estate or purchase existing mortgage securities. The revenues of a mortgage REIT come from the interest earned on the mortgage loans. *Hybrid REITs* are a combination of equity and mortgage REITs. With a hybrid REIT, in other words, an investor can invest in a combination of real estate and mortgages.

REAL RATE OF RETURN

Real rate of return refers to the annual return on an investment after the inflation rate has been subtracted. The real rate of return changes with economic changes, tastes, and preference; consequently, it is usually expressed by percentage.

RETAINED EARNINGS

Also called *undistributed profits, accumulated earnings,* or *earned surplus,* retain earnings are net profits accumulated over the life of a business after dividends have been paid. They are reflected in an increase in the stockholders' equity reported on a company's balance sheet.

Retained earnings are available for reinvestment into the business or for paying off debts.

RETURN ON EQUITY (ROE)

ROE, also known as *return on investment,* is a percentage measure of the overall profits earned by a firm during a particular period. ROE allows shareholders to judge how efficiently the company is employing their money. It is closely followed by investors because of its direct link to the profits, growth, and dividends of the company. Comparisons of ROE for current and prior periods reveal trends, and comparsions with other companies show how well a company is holding against its competitors.

ROE relates profits to shareholders' equity:

$$ROE = \frac{\text{net profit after taxes}}{\text{Shareholders' equity}}$$

ROE shows the annual payout to investors, who usually look for companies with ROEs that are high and growing. A business that creates much shareholder equity is considered a sound investment because the original investors will be repaid.

ROE affords investors an excellent sense of whether they will receive a decent return on equity and also allows them to assess management's ability to get the job done.

Shareholder's equity can be found on a company's balance sheet; it is simply the difference between total assets and total liabilities. The way that investors most often see shareholders' equity displayed is as a per-share value called "book value." Book value is the amount of shareholder's equity per share, or the accounting book value of the business outside of its market value or intrinsic economic value.

RISK

The chance that the return from an investment will differ from what is expected. A drop in value of invested capital can be caused by many factors, including inflation, interest rate changess, default, politics, liquidity, and call provisions.

The investment world has to balance risk and return. Risky investments offer the hope of receiving a higher return than risk-free investments. Risk is not wholly bad: certain investors try to avoid risk by making safe investments, only to discover that they have declined in value. An investor can instead moderate risk through diversification and over time.

Examples

1. *Business risk:* Level of uncertainty associated with an investment's earnings and its ability to pay the returns owed investors.

2. *Financial risk:* Level of uncertainty of payment connected to the mix of debt and equity used to finance a firm or property; the larger the proportion of debt financing, the greater the risk.

3. *Inflation risk:* Risk that value of the assets will decrease as inflation reduces the purchasing power of a currency.

4. *Purchasing power risk:* Possibility that changing price levels in the economy will damage investment returns.

5. *Interest rate risk:* Possibility that changes in interest rates will harm a security's value.

6. *Liquidity risk:* The possible risk of not being able to liquidate an asset at a reasonable price.

7. *Mortgage risk:* Risk that a mortgagee will not make payments on time or follow the terms of the agreement.

8. *Economic risk:* Risk that a financed project will not generate sufficient profits to cover expenses such as operating costs or to repay debt obligations.

9. *Market risk:* Risk that investment returns will decline because of market factors independent of the given security.

10. *Tax risk:* Risk of an unfavorable change in tax laws that will affect the value of an investment.

11. *Event risk:* Risk that an unexpected event will have a significant effect on the underlying value of a share.

S

S&P/TSX COMPOSITE INDEX

Also known as the *TSE Composite Index,* the S&P/TSX Composite Index measures the market changes of more than 200 stocks traded on the Toronto Exchange market (TSX). It accounts for approximately 70 percent of the total market capitalization of firms listed on the TSX.

The price of each stock in the index is evaluated on the total shares outstanding, meaning that large-capitalization companies have a stronger effect on the index.

There are fourteen major group indices, including energy, financials, and income trusts.

SAVINGS AND LOANS (S&L) ASSOCIATION

S&Ls are financial institutions that accept savings deposits from private investors, provide mortgage loans to the public, and pay dividends. An S&L association is usually mutually held, meaning that both borrowers and depositors have voting rights within the institution and the ability to regulate its financial and administrative goals.

SAVINGS BONDS

Also known as *U.S. savings bonds* or *Series EE savings bonds,* savings bonds are similar to Treasury bonds in that they are U.S. government bonds issued at face value. Even the smallest investor can purchase them, because they come in small denominations (from $50 to $10,000), have no transaction costs, and are absolutely protected in terms of payment of interest and principal.

Because they are a contract between the government and the bond-holder, savings bonds are not marketable; after being purchased from the government, they cannot be bought or sold. Thus, no secondary market exists for this type of bond.

Among the advantages of purchasing a savings bond are the tax benefits. Similar to any other Treasury bond, they are exempt from state and local taxes; in addition, in the case of savings bonds, all federal taxes are postponed until the bond is exchanged. In other words, no taxes are paid until the money can be accessed, even though interest accumulates. Moreover, if the money is used to pay the tuition expenses of a family member, then the interest earned may be exempt from federal taxes. Each bond is a registered security for which the Bureau of the Public Debt maintains a record.

SECURITIES

Securities are instruments that represent ownership or the right to acquire or sell ownership. Securities also represent the debt of a corporation. A security is effectively anything that can have a value or be traded.

Examples of securities include notes, stocks, preferred shares, bonds, debentures, options, or any investment or financial asset.

SECURITIES AND EXCHANGE COMMISSION (SEC)

The SEC is the agency in charge of administering federal securities laws and overseeing securities to protect investors and promote full disclosure. The SEC has the power to regulate the organized securities exchanges and the over-the-counter (OTC) market by extending disclosure requirements to outstanding securities. The SEC covers the organized exchanges and the OTC market, their members, brokers, and dealers, and the securities traded in the market. It has four main divisions: Corporate Finance, Market Regulations, Enforcement, and Investment and Management.

SECURITIES INVESTOR PROTECTION CORPORATION (SIPC)

The SIPC is a nonprofit organization created by an act of Congress to protect the clients of brokerage firms that are forced into bankruptcy. The members of SIPC are all of those brokers and dealers registered with the Securities Exchange Commission created in 1934, members of securities exchanges, and most NASD members.

SIPC provides brokerage customers with up to $500,000 insurance coverage for cash and securities in the event of brokerage bankruptcy. The cash coverage is limited to $100,000. Although the SIPC protects against brokerage economic failure, it does not protect against investment losses.

SELLING

To sell is to transfer ownership of a stock or other type of asset in exchange for money and/or value.

Insider selling: This is the selling of a company's stock by individual directors or executives. This practice is illegal.

Cross-selling: A strategy of pushing new products onto existing clientele based on their past purchases. Cross-selling aims to decrease the possibility of customers buying from a competitor.

Selling flat: Selling when a price has neither risen nor fallen.

Selling hedge: The sale of futures contracts to protect against a possible decline in the price of securities.

SHAREHOLDERS

Also known as *stockholders,* shareholders are individuals who own shares of stock in a corporation or mutual fund. A shareholder is usually entitled to four basic rights:

1. A claim on a share of the company's undivided assets in proportion to the number of shares held.
2. Proportionate voting power in the election of directors and in other business.

3. Dividends declared by the board of directors.
4. A preemptive right to subscribe to additional stock offerings before they are available to the general public (some restrictions may apply).

SHORT-TERM INVESTMENTS

Short-term investments have a maturity of one year or less and are the most traditional type of investments, perfect for investors who have a short period in which to invest. The rates of these investments can be volatile, depending on the market's performance.

SPECULATOR

A speculator is someone who attempts to profit from selling and buying contracts by anticipating future price adjustments. The speculator assumes market prices and adds liquidity and capital to future markets. Speculators may purchase stocks from a mutual fund or volatile shares and hold on to them for a short time to obtain a profit.

STATE REGULATORS

Regulators of the fifty U.S. states protect the buyers of securities sold in their state. State regulators screen all securities offerings documents to ensure that all of the necessary information has been disclosed and that the deal is not fraudulent. State regulators cannot predict an investment's potential, but they do reject offerings that seem dishonest.

The prescreening process is known as the *"blue-sky" process,* and potential investors should ask their state regulator whether the bond or stock they are interested in has passed the blue-sky process.

STOCK

Also known as an *equity, equity securities,* or *corporate stock,* a stock represents a share of ownership in a business and a claim on a proportional share in the corporation's assets and gains, as determined by the number of shares a shareholder posseses divided by the total number of outstanding shares.

Most stock provides shareholders with voting rights in certain corporate decisions. Only corporations issue stocks.

The benefits of stocks make them appealing to corporations and individuals. Traditionally, stocks were issued as certificates, but they are now electronic to avoid loss, damage, or theft of the certificate.

STOCK INDEX

Stock index is an index based of the share prices of a number of representative stocks. Examples are the Dow Jones Industrials, S&P 500, NASDAQ composite, and Russell 2000.

Indexes are very useful for benchmarking portfolios and for determining the market return used in the CAPM (capital asset pricing model). As some portfolios are too broad to measure easily, stock indexes have been created to provide investors with an indicator of the overall market's performance.

STRIPS

STRIP is an acronym for separate trading of registered interest and principal of securities. STRIPS are bonds, issued by the U.S. Treasury, whose two components, interest and repayment of principal, are sold separately as zero-coupon bonds.

STRIPS can be purchased and held only through financial institutions and government securities brokers and dealers. They are popular investments for individual retirement accounts, 401k-type savings plans, and other income-tax-advantaged accounts that permit earnings to accumulate without immediate tax consequences.

SYSTEMATIC RISK

Also known as market risk or nondiversifiable risk, systematic risk is the risk of war, inflation, and political or other events impacting large portions of the market. It can decrease the value of an investment over time. It is common to a number of assets and liabilities.

Systematic risk cannot be entirely diversified because if the market is affected it will affect all stocks equally, and thus the entire economy. However, asset allocation and diversification provide some mesure of protection from systematic risk because different areas of the market tend to perform badly or to underperform at different times.

TAX

A fee charged by the government on a product, income, or activity and imposed on people, organizations, or properties. A direct tax is one imposed on personal or corporate income; an indirect tax is one imposed on the price of a good or service.

The purpose of taxation is to finance the government's everyday expenditures. One of the most important uses is to finance public services.

Examples

Income tax: Annual tax levied by the federal government, most states, and some cities on an individual's salary or an organization's net profit.

Sales tax: Tax levied by a state or city on the retail price of an item. Sales tax is collected by the vendor.

Self-employment tax: Social Security tax paid by a self-employed individual.

Social Security tax: Federal tax imposed equally on the employer and the employee and used to pay for Social Security programs.

Nonresident alien tax: Tax withheld from the income received by foreign individuals or corporations.

Inheritance tax: Tax imposed on the privilege of inheriting something. Inheritance tax, which is paid by the recipient.

Estate tax: Tax imposed on the transfer of property from a deceased person to his or her heirs.

Luxury tax: Tax levied on products considered nonessential.

Sin tax: Tax imposed on items considered vices, such as alcohol and tobacco.

Other Terms and Definitions

Regressive tax: Tax that takes a larger percentage of the income of low-income people than of high-income people.

Progressive tax: A tax system in which those with higher incomes pay more taxes than those with lower incomes.

Flat tax: A system in which all income levels are taxed at the same rate.

TAX-DEFERRED RETIREMENT ACCOUNTS

A tax-deferred investment in which taxes become due only when the investor takes possession of the investment or it is sold. Investors have realized that tax-deferred investments are among the best ways to save for retirement. Tax-deferred investing lets a person keep money that would have been paid in taxes, leaving a greater amount available for investing.

In some cases, the government allows taxable income to be reduced by the amount of the contribution to a tax-deferred retirement plan. This means people can still have the same amount of money in their pockets after they invest what they would have paid the government into a tax-deferred retirement plan. The amount saved will depend on the marginal tax rate (10, 15, 25, 28, 33, or 35 percent). The higher an investor's marginal tax rate, the more he or she benefits from pretax dollar contributions and tax-deferred earnings.

Most tax-deferred accounts carry a penalty for withdrawing the money before age fifty-nine.

Among the retirement plans the government allows as tax-deferred investments are employer-sponsored plans, plans for self-employed persons, and individual retirement accounts (IRAs).

TAX REFORM ACT OF 1986

This Act was federal legislation that made significant changes to the U.S. tax system. Among these changes were

* the elimination of the preferential tax treatment of capital gains;
* an increase in the standard deduction indexed to inflation starting in 1989;

- restrictions on the deductibility of individual retirement account contributions;
- allowing investment interest expenses to be offset against investment income, dollar for dollar, without limitation;
- modification of many of the rules for taxation of the foreign operations of U.S. multinational companies;
- liberalized requirements for employee vesting in a company's qualified pension plan and changes to other rules affecting employee benefit plans;
- repealing of the deduction for two-earner married couples;
- repealing of income averaging for all taxpayers;
- a lowering of the top rehabilitation tax credit from 25 to 20 percent; and
- amended rules for qualifying as a real estate investment trust (REIT) and for the taxation of REITs.

TERM LIFE INSURANCE

This is a type of life insurance that provides a stated benefit upon the policyholder's death. Term life insurance is written for a specific period of time and requires the policyholder to pay only the cost of the protection against death.

Each time the insurance is renewed, the premium is higher because the insured is older and more likely to die.

Term life insurance is less expensive than whole-life insurance.

TICKER TAPE

Also known as *tape,* ticker tape is a computerized device that displays to investors all over the world symbols, prices, and volume information for each transaction on the major exchanges.

On television business programs such as CNBC a ticker tape appears at the bottom of the screen (Figure 4).

- *Ticker symbol:* The character used to identify the company.
- *Shares traded:* Volume for the trade being quoted (K = 1,000, M = 1,000.000, and B = 1,000,000,000).

- *Price traded:* Price per share or the latest bid price.
- *Change direction:* Indication of whether the stock is trading higher or lower than the previous day's closing price.
- *Change amount:* The difference in price from the previous day.

MSFT	5K@	61.25	▼	1.35
↑	↑	↑	↑	↑
Ticker Symbol	Shares Traded	Price Traded	Change Direction	Change Amount

FIGURE 4. Example of a ticker tape.

Some television shows use a color scheme to indicate how the stock is changing. For instance, green indicates that the stock is trading higher than at the previous day's close; red shows that the stock is trading lower than at the previous day's close; and blue or white indicates that there has been no change since the previous day's close.

TREASURY BILLS (T-BILLS)

Short-term securities with maturities of one year or less issued at a discount from face value. T-bills are sold on a discount basis. They are regarded as the safest of all investments and are highly liquid. Treasury bills are the primary instruments used by the Federal Reserve to regulate money supply through open-market operations.

T-bills are issued in a minimum denomination of $10,000, with $5,000 increments above $10,000. An individual can purchase T-bills directly in weekly Treasury auctions or indirectly through local commercial banks, securities dealers, or brokers who buy bills for investors on a commission basis. Investors can also purchase T-bills in the secondary market though banks and brokers.

TREASURY BONDS (T-BONDS)

Also known as governments or treasuries, T-bonds are U.S. Treasury debt securities issued with maturities of more than ten years (usually thirty-year maturities). T-bonds are the best-known type of bond in the fixed-income market. They are all backed by the full faith and credit of the U.S. government. Moreover, all Treasury obligations are very popular among individuals and investors in the United States and overseas because of their liquidity.

The interest on T-bonds is paid semiannually at a fixed coupon rate. The bonds are exempt from state and local taxes and come in denominations from $1,000 to $1 million.

TREASURY INFLATION-
PROTECTED SECURITIES (TIPS)

TIPS are a type of security similar to Treasury bonds, except that the principal and coupon payments are adjusted to eliminate the effects of inflation, TIPS are intended to protect investors against fluctuations in inflation by linking the principal amount to the consumer price index.

TIPS have a fixed coupon (interest rate) and mature on a specified date in the future. They are one of two inflation-indexed securities sold by the U.S. Treasury, the other being Series I savings bonds.

TREASURY NOTES (T-NOTES)

T-notes are similar to Treasury bonds, with the exception that they are intermediate securities with maturities from one to ten years. T-notes are backed by the full faith and credit of the U.S. government; thus, they are viewed as having no credit risk. The denominations range from $1,000 to $1 million or more.

T-notes are issued as bills, and the yield of the ten-year T-note is usually used as the benchmark interest rate. They earn and pay a fixed rate of interest every six months until maturity.

The government arranges an auction to gather bids to price the debt and set the interest rate payable. After the debt has been sold at the auction, it trades actively in a secondary market where the price of the T-note rises when interest rates fall and vice versa.

T-notes can be bought from the U.S. Treasury or through a bank broker. An investor who buys them through the U.S. Treasury can place either a competitive bid (specifying the yield the investor will accept at auction) or a noncompetitive bid (agreeing to accept whatever yield is determined at auction).

T-notes are used to finance education or as a supplementary retirement income. An investor can sell a T-note before or at maturity at the existing market rate. For more information, see http://www.public debt.treas.gov/sec/sectrdir.htm.

TREASURY SECURITIES

Securities issued by the Treasury Department of the U.S. government, Treasury securities are negotiable debt obligations issued with different maturities. The income used to purchase such securities is exempt from state and local taxes; however, federal taxes are payable on the interest earned.

Treasury securities are issued to pay for government projects. As they are backed up by the full faith and credit of the government, they are considered low-risk investments. They are sold in the primary market by the government, but they are marketable securities; that is, they can be purchased through a broker in the secondary market. The difference between the two types of purchases is that the government does not charge a fee, whereas the broker does.

Three types of Treasury securities are issued by the government: T-bonds, T-notes, and T-bills. The difference is in their maturity and, in some instances, the denominations.

The Treasury securities issued today are not callable: they continue to accumulate interest until the date of maturity. A potential downside is that if interest rates increase during the term of the security, the money invested will be earning less interest than it could earn elsewhere.

TREASURY STOCK

Also known as *treasury shares* or *required stock,* Tresury stock is reacquired by the issuing company and available for retirement or resale. It is issued but not outstanding; it does not have voting rights attached, and it does not pay accruals or dividends.

Treasury stocks are created to provide an alternative to paying taxable dividends and to allow for the exercise of stock options and warrants and the conversion of convertible securities.

TRUSTS AND LOANS

Trust: An arrangement that authorizes one or more people (the trustees) to look after and administer the assets, such as property and money, of another person or people, who are known as the beneficiaries.

Loan: An advance of money from a lender to a borrower over a period of time. The borrower has to repay the loan plus interest either at intervals or at the end of the loan period.

UNEMPLOYMENT RATE

This is a monthly indicator of the percentage of individuals who are seeking employment. The rate is caluclated by the Bureau of Labor Statistics.

An unemployment rate of 4 to 6 percent is considered healthy in a society. If the rate is lower, it is considered inflationary. If the rate is higher, it will threaten a decrease in consumer spending. Variations in the rate are due to changes in the economic activity of a nation.

UNIT INVESTMENT TRUST (UIT)

A UIT is a type of mutual fund that holds a fixed portfolio of securities, such as corporate, municipal, or government bonds, mortgage-backed securities, common stock, and preferred stock. For a sales charge, which is usually 4 percent for municipal bond trusts and 1 to 2 percent for equity trusts, brokers sell units to investors. The trusts expire when the bonds mature.

The units are listed on an exchange and they are traded in the same way as stocks. The best-known example of a UIT is the Standard & Poor's Depositary Receipt.

Similar to stocks, UITs can be sold or bought at any time and in some instances are comparable to an index mutual fund. The value of a UIT is usually $1,000, and it is sold in the secondary market.

V

VARIABLE ANNUITY

This is an annuity contract into which money is invested in installments or as a lump sum. Investors can pick the level of risk they find acceptable; the higher the level of risk they accept, the higher the potential rate of return.

Variable annuity contracts are commonly used as a retirement tool because they provide future payments to the investor. The amount received will depend on the performance of the portfolio's shares. The rate of return from a variable annuity can be looked at as being composed of the rate of return from a high-risk, high-return investment and the compensation for the investor's early death.

An individual can invest in a mutual fund or in some money market funds (with corporate or government bonds in them) that have lower levels of risk but lower rates of return.

VARIABLE LIFE INSURANCE

Variable life insurance is life insurance that allows policyholders to invest the cash value of their policy in stocks, bonds, or money market portfolios, so the payment depends on the investment made by the investor.

Registered representatives of a broker or dealer licensed by the National Association of Securities Dealers (NASD) and registered with the Securities and Exchange Commission can sell this type of insurance.

As with a whole life insurance, the annual premium is fixed. However, because the policyholder bears the risk of securities investments, the cash values and death benefits will rise if the investment does well and fall if the investment drops in value. The benefits are taxed not as individual income but as taxable estate income.

$$\boxed{W}$$

WILSHIRE TOTAL MARKET INDEX

This is an index similar to the S&P 500 and NASDAQ composite index that measures the performance of all U.S.-headquartered equity securities with readily available price data. It measures the total dollar value of more than 6,500 actively traded stocks, including all those listed on the New York Stock Exchange and the AMEX, together with active over-the-counter stocks. Among the advantages of this index are that it is the most diversified index in the world and that it covers almost all public companies in the United States. However, it does not include foreign issues, ADRs, or any stock without readily available price data.

The Wilshire 500 index is reported daily in the *Wall Street Journal*. Funds that represent this index can be purchased; however, the Wilshire 500 has a relatively high ratio for an index fund.

WITHHOLDING TAX

Also known as a *withholding,* a withholding tax is a deduction from salary payments and other compensation to provide for an individual's tax liability. Federal income taxes and Social Security contributions are withheld from paychecks and are deposited in a Treasury tax and loan account with a bank.

Anyone who starts a new job has to fill out a form W-4, declaring his or her filling status and the number of allowances claimed.

Y

YIELD

The return on an investor's capital investment, yield is the percentage paid on a common preferred stock in the form of dividends. For a bond, yield is the return that takes into account the total of annual interest payments, the purchase price, the redemption value, and the amount of time remaining until maturity. For a lending, yield is the total amount of money earned from a loan. For taxes, yield is the revenue received by a government entity.

YIELD-TO-MATURITY

Also known as *promised yield,* yield-to-maturity is a concept is widely used to define the rate of return an investor will receive if a long-term bond is held until its maturity date. It takes into consideration the purchase price, redemption value, time to maturity, coupon yield, and time between interest payments.

Yield-to-maturity can be approximated using a bond value table or a programmable calculator.

Z

ZERO-COUPON BONDS

A zero-coupon is a bond with no coupons that is sold at a deep discount to its face value, and at the maturity date is greater than the initial investment, thus its closing face value.

Zero-coupon bonds pay no interest; actually, they pay nothing until the issue matures. Thus, among the most appealing features of zero-coupon bonds is that they are free from reinvestment risk. Another advantage is that the cheaper a zero-coupon bond is, the higher the return for the investor.

However, zero-coupon bonds have some disadvantages. First, if the rates of zero-coupons become high, the investor cannot partake in the higher return. Second, zero-coupon bonds are subject to price volatility; if the market rates increase, for example, a considerable capital loss will result as the price of zero-coupon bonds falls. Third, the IRS requires zero-coupon investors to report interest as it accumulates, depsite the absence of any cash flow. Finally, zero-coupon bonds are somewhat illiquid.

Corporations, municipalities, and federal agencies issue zero-coupons. In some cases, U.S. Treasury bonds can be bought as zero-coupon securities known as *Treasure STRIPs* or *STRIP-Ts*.

ZERO-COUPON CONVERTIBLES

Also known as *split-coupon bonds,* zero-coupon convertibles are zero-coupon bonds issued by a corporation that can be converted into a common stock when the stock reaches a predetermined price. They are suitable for trading at a small premium over conversion value and provide a lower yield to maturity than nonconvertible bonds.

Moreover, zero-coupon convertibles are usually municipal bonds, which can be converted into interest-bearing bonds at some time before maturity under certain circumstances.

Bibliography

Online Investment Dictionaries

Businessweek.com

http://bwnt.businessweek.com/Glossary
Dictionary providing specific definitions of financial and business terminology

The CFTC Glossary

http://www.cftc.gov/opa/glossary/opaglossary_a.htm
Compilation of terms used in the financial world for the general public

Insure.com

http://info.insure.com/glossary/new_results.cfm?termsearch-a
Dictionary providing basic definitions of common financial terms for the general
public

Investorwords.com

http://www.investorwords.com/cgi-bin/letter.cgi?
Online dictionary providing basic information about business terms and, in some instances, examples

Merrill Lynch Glossary

http://www.fs.ml.com/help/glossary.asp?term=a
Dictionary providing substantial definitions, as well as short definitions for begin-
ner investors

Foundation Web Sites

Fannie Mae Foundation

http://www.fanniemaefoundation.org
Fannie Mae Foundation's Web site, which provides comprehensive information regarding the organization

Ginnie Mae

http://www.ginniemae.gov
Main Web site of Ginnie Mae, which includes mortgage information for investors
and issuers

NASDAQ

http://www.nasdaqtrader.com
Provides daily information of trades and NASDAQ's market changes

U.S. Securities and Exchange Commission

http://www.sec.gov
Information about the SEC, definitions, regulations, and forms

Wells Fargo

http://www.wellsfargo.com
Information about banking, investing, and loans, with definitions of key terms

Magazines, Newspapers, and Charts

Financial Guide

http://www.financial-guide.ch
Financial site providing definitions and charts of the learning curve of markets, investment, and derivations

Forbes.com

http://www.forbes.com
Web site of the magazine, with information on market activity; it also has a glossary

Incredible Charts

http://www.incrediblecharts.com
Selection of different charts and definitions of various financial transactions

The Washington Post

http://www.washingtonpost.com/wp-srv/business
An online version of the business and financial publication

Reference Books

Boone, Louis E., Kurtz, David L., Hearth, Douglas. (2000). *Planning Your Financial Future.* Orlando, FL: Dryden Press.

Daunten, Carl A., Welshans, Merlet. (1970). *Principles of Finance,* Third Edition. Cincinatti, OH: Southwestern Publishing Co.

Downes, John, Goodman, Jordan Elliot. (2003). *Finance & Investment Handbook,* Sixth Edition. Hayppauge, NY: Barron's.

Gitman, Lawrence J., Joehnk, Michael D. (1999). *Fundamentals of Investing,* Seventh Edition. New York: Addison-Wesley.

————. (1999). *Personal Financial Planning.* Orlando, FL: Dryden Press.

Hadjimichalakis, Michael G, Hadjimichalakis, Karma G. (1995). *Contemporary Money, Banking, and Financial Markets: Theory and Practice.* Chicago, IL: Irwin.

Kapoor, Jack R., Dlabay, Les R., Hughes, Robert J. (1999). *Personal Finance,* Fifth Edition. Irwin/McGraw-Hill.

Mishkin, Frederic S. (2001). *The Economics of Money, Banking, and Financial Markets.* New York: Addison Wesley.

Rutgers Cooperative Extension (2000). *Investing for Your Future.* Brunswick, NJ: The State University of New Jersey.

Index

Page numbers followed by the letter "f" indicate figures.

A stock, 10
Absolute return, hedge fund, 32-33
Accumulated earnings, 60
Active strategy, 3
Agricultural products, as commodities,
    8-9, 8f
American Century, 23
American exercise, 50
AMEX (American Stock Exchange),
    41-42
Asset-backed bonds, 5

B stock, 10
Balance sheet, 24, 25f
Bank deposit agreement (BDA), 31
Bank investment contract (BIC), 31
Bermudan exercise, 50
Big Board (NYSE), 47
"Blue-sky" process, 66
Boeing, 30
Bond
    corporate, types of, 5-6
    duration of, 13-14
    fixed-income investment and,
        20-21
    types of, 5
Book value, 61
Brokers, 47, 48-49
Bureau of the Public Debt, 64
Business risk, 61

Calculations
    beta measurements, 4f
    EPS, 15
    equivalent taxable yield, 18
    Macaulay duration, 13-14
    municipal bonds, 44
    return on equity, 60
Call option, 50
Callable bonds, 5
Capital lease, 40
Cash flow statement, 24
Change amount, ticker tape, 72
Change direction, ticker tape, 72
China, emerging market, 16
Commodity Exchange Act, 8
Company analysis, 24
Compound interest, 26
Consumer Price Index (CPI), 39
Convertible preferred stock, 53
Corporate bonds, 5, 20
Corporate diversification, 12
Corporate Finance, SEC, 64
Corporate stock, 66-67
Cross-selling, 65
Cumulative preferred stock, 53
Current assets, 3

Debenture bonds, 5
Deferred equities, 10
Derivatives, 26
Direct financing lease, 40

Direct issues, mortgage, 55
Direct tax, 69
Diversification, hedge fund, 34
Dow Jones Averages, 42, 67
Dreyfus, 23

Earned surplus, 60
Earnings multiple, 54-55
Economic risk, 62
Enforcement (SEC), 64
EPS (earnings per share), 15-16
Equity REITs, 59
Equity securities, 66-67
ESOP (employee stock ownership
    plan), 16-17
ESPP (employee stock purchase plan),
    17-18
Essential purpose bond, 56
Estate tax, 69
European exercise, 50
Event risk, 62
Exchange (NYSE), 47
Expense statement, 37

Family of funds, 23
Federal Home Loan Mortgage
    Corporations, 22
Federal Housing Administration
    (FHA), 30
Fees, broker, 48
Fidelity, 23
Financial lease, 40
Financial risk, 61
Fixed assets, 3
Flat tax, 70
Flexibility, hedge fund, 33
Floating rate bonds, 5
Following the market, 7-8
401K plan, 21, 58
403B plan, 21, 58
408K plan, 21-22
457 plan, 58
Franklin Resources, 30
Fund manager, hedge fund, 33-34
Futures market, commodities and, 8

GDR (global depository receipt), 28-29
General obligation bonds, 43-44
General-purpose money funds, 43
GIC (guaranteed investment contract),
    31
GNMA, 28, 29-30
GNMA 1, 28
GNMA 2, 28
GNMA midgets, 28
G-O (general obligation) bond, 27
Government bonds, 5, 20
Government securities money funds,
    30, 43
GTC (good-til-canceled) order, 29

Health care, retirement benefit, 51
Hybrid REITs, 60

Imperfect hedge, 34
Income statement, 24, 37
Income tax, 69
Indirect tax, 69
Individual diversification, 12
Inflation, 38-39
Inflation risk, 61
Inheritance tax, 69
Insider selling, 65
Intel, 30
Interest rate risk, 62
Investment, 38-39
Investment and Management (SEC), 64
IRA (individual retirement account), 38

Junk bond, 35

Keogh plan, 57

Leading P/E, 54
Leverage, option contract, 50

Life insurance
    term, 71
    variable, 77
Life-only annuity, 36
Liquidity risk, 62
Lithuania, emerging market, 16
Load fund, 23
Loan, 75
Long-term gains, 7
Luxury tax, 69

Macaulay's formula, 13-14
Magellan, Fidelity, 49
Market Regulations (SEC), 64
Market risk, 62, 67-68
Merrill Lynch, 23, 48
Metals, as investment, 52
Mexico, emerging market, 16
Microsoft, 30
Money funds, 42-43
Mortgage
    Freddie Mac, 22
    Ginnie Mae, 28
    Government National Mortgage
        Association (GNMA), 29-30
    mortgage-backed securities, 43
    private mortgage participation
        certificate, 55
Mortgage bonds, 5
Mortgage pass-through security, 51
Mortgage REITs, 59-60
Mortgage risk, 62
Motorola, 30
Municipal bonds, 5, 20, 43-44
Munis, 43-44
Mutual funds, 12, 44-45

NASD (National Association of
        Securities Dealers), 42, 46, 77
NASDAQ composite, 67
NASDAQ National Market, 46
NASDAQ Small Cap Market, 46

National Association of Securities
        Dealers Automated
        Quotations (NASDAQ), 46
Net asset value (NAV), 49
Nominal value, 20
Nonconvertible preferred stock, 53
Noncumulative preferred stock, 53
Nondiversifiable risk, 67-68
Nonrefund annuity, 36
Nonresident alien tax, 69
NYSE (New York Stock Exchange), 47

Open order, 29
Open outcry system, 26, 47
Open-end fund, 44, 49
Open-end lease, 40
Operating lease, 40
Operating statement, 37
Over-the-counter market, 64

Paine Webber, 23, 48
Par value, 20
Participating preferred stock, 53
Pass-through, 28, 51, 55
P/E (price-earnings) ration, 54-55
Perfect hedge, 34
Period certain annuity, 36
PPI (producer price index), 55-56
Preference shares, 52-53
Pre-refunded bonds, 5
Price, bond, 14
Price gaps, 27
Price traded, 72
Principal amount, 20
Profits per share, 15-16
Progressive tax, 70
Promised yield, 79
Protection, option contract, 50
Public activity bond, 56
Public and Indian Housing (PIH),
        Department of Housing and
        Urban Development, 30
Public offering, 48

Purchasing power risk, 61
Put option, 50, 56

Regressive tax, 70
REIT (real estate investment trust), 59-60
Renter's lease, 40
Required stock, 74-75
Retirement
    benefits, 51-52
    401K plan, 21, 58
    403B plan, 21, 58
    408K plan, 21-22
    457 plan, 58
    nonqualified plans, 47
    qualified plans, 57-58
    tax-deferred accounts, 70
Return on investment, 60-61
Revenue bonds, 44
Risk, reducing
    market, alpha, 1
    market, beta, 4, 4f
    retirement, annuity, 2
ROE (return on equity), 60-61
Roth IRA, 38
Rural Housing Administration (RHA), 30
Russell 2000, 67

Sales tax, 69
Sales-type lease, 40
SARSSEP plan, 21-22
Scudder, 23
Securities and Exchange Commission (SEC), 42, 48, 64
Self-Employed Individuals Tax Retirement Act, 57
Self-employment tax, 69
Selling flat, 65
Selling hedge, 65
SEPs, 38, 57
Series EE savings bonds, 63
Shares traded, 71

Short-term gains, 7
SIMPLEs, 38
Sin tax, 69
Single-life annuity, 36
SIPC (Securities Investor Protection Corporation), 65
Skill-based investment, hedge fund, 33
S&Ls (savings and loans), 63
Smith Barney, 23, 48
Social Security tax, 69
South Africa, emerging market, 16
Split-coupon bonds, 80
Stable policy, 3
Standard & Poor's Depositary Receipt, 76
Standard & Poor's (S&P) Indexes, 42, 67
Statement of profit and loss, 37
Stock option, 56
Stockholders, common stock, 9-10, 65-66
Straight-life annuity, 36
Strike price, 50
STRIP-Ts, 80
Strong, 23
Subordinated debentures, 6

T. Rowe Price, 23
Tape, 71-72, 72f
Tax risk, 62
Tax-exempt money funds, 43
T-bill, 72, 74
T-bond, 72-73, 74
Term insurance, 40
Ticker symbol, 71
TIPS (Treasury inflation-protected securities), 73
T-notes, 73-74
Toronto Exchange market (TSX), 63
Trading, commodities, 8
Traditional government purpose bond, 56
Traditional IRA, 38
Treasure STRIPs, 80

Treasury Inflation-Protected Securities
(TIPS), 38-39
Treasury shares, 74-75
True lease, 40
Trust, 75
Trustee structure, mortgage, 55
TSE Composite Index, 63

UIT (unit investment trust), 76
Undistributed profits, 60
Universal insurance, 40
U.S. Bureau of Labor Statistics, 55
U.S. savings bonds, 63

Vanguard, 23
Vanguard 500, 38, 49
Veterans Administration (VA), 30

Well's Fargo Non-Qualified Retirement
Program, 47
Whipsaw, 7-8
Whole life insurance, 40
Withholding, 78

Zero-coupon bonds, 6

Order a copy of this book with this form or online at:
http://www.haworthpress.com/store/product.asp?sku=5689

CONCISE ENCYCLOPEDIA OF INVESTING

_____ in hardbound at $29.95 (ISBN-13: 978-0-7890-2343-8; ISBN-10: 0-7890-2343-1)
_____ in softbound at $19.95 (ISBN-13: 978-0-7890-2344-5; ISBN-10: 0-7890-2344-X)

84 pages plus index • Includes illustrations

Or order online and use special offer code HEC25 in the shopping cart.

COST OF BOOKS_____

POSTAGE & HANDLING_____
(US: $4.00 for first book & $1.50
for each additional book)
(Outside US: $5.00 for first book
& $2.00 for each additional book)

SUBTOTAL_____

IN CANADA: ADD 6% GST_____

STATE TAX_____
(NJ, NY, OH, MN, CA, IL, IN, PA, & SD
residents, add appropriate local sales tax)

FINAL TOTAL_____
(If paying in Canadian funds,
convert using the current
exchange rate, UNESCO
coupons welcome)

☐ **BILL ME LATER:** (Bill-me option is good on
US/Canada/Mexico orders only; not good to
jobbers, wholesalers, or subscription agencies.)
☐ Check here if billing address is different from
shipping address and attach purchase order and
billing address information.

Signature _____

☐ **PAYMENT ENCLOSED: $**_____

☐ **PLEASE CHARGE TO MY CREDIT CARD.**

☐ Visa ☐ MasterCard ☐ AmEx ☐ Discover
☐ Diner's Club ☐ Eurocard ☐ JCB

Account # _____

Exp. Date_____

Signature_____

Prices in US dollars and subject to change without notice.

NAME_____
INSTITUTION_____
ADDRESS_____
CITY_____
STATE/ZIP_____
COUNTRY_____ COUNTY (NY residents only)_____
TEL_____ FAX_____
E-MAIL_____

May we use your e-mail address for confirmations and other types of information? ☐ Yes ☐ No
We appreciate receiving your e-mail address and fax number. Haworth would like to e-mail or fax special
discount offers to you, as a preferred customer. **We will never share, rent, or exchange your e-mail address
or fax number.** We regard such actions as an invasion of your privacy.

Order From Your Local Bookstore or Directly From
The Haworth Press, Inc.
10 Alice Street, Binghamton, New York 13904-1580 • USA
TELEPHONE: 1-800-HAWORTH (1-800-429-6784) / Outside US/Canada: (607) 722-5857
FAX: 1-800-895-0582 / Outside US/Canada: (607) 771-0012
E-mail to: orders@haworthpress.com

For orders outside US and Canada, you may wish to order through your local
sales representative, distributor, or bookseller.
For information, see http://haworthpress.com/distributors

(Discounts are available for individual orders in US and Canada only, not booksellers/distributors.)

PLEASE PHOTOCOPY THIS FORM FOR YOUR PERSONAL USE.
http://www.HaworthPress.com   BOF06